FEAR NO DISTANCE

A Journey to Life without Limits

DANIELLE GRABOL

Susanna Lagoon™ Books

SUSANNA LAGOON™ Books
An imprint of J. K. Eckert and Company, Inc.
Nokomis, FL 34275
www.jkeckert.com

Cover photograph by Colin Cross

ISBN: 978-0-9913571-8-5

To all the strong-willed little girls with messy hair who like to jump in puddles. Please never stop being different in the most wondrous of ways.

Contents

Acknowledgments

Writing a book was hard, much harder than I ever anticipated. I want to thank everyone who has asked me, "When are you writing a book?" and encouraged me to share my story. I am continuously humbled that people are interested in hearing about my adventures.

This book would not have come to fruition without the support and contribution of my friend Dusty Scott. Thank you for asking questions and pressing me to share more.

I am deeply appreciative of my Aunt Jenn and Uncle Jeff Eckert (J.K. Eckert & Co.). They not only edited my book, they also designed the interior and covers. Plus, they answered countless questions about the publishing process. Your expertise and help was greatly appreciated.

To Dr. Warren Davidson: you spoke to me candidly and honestly in your examining room in 2005. I will forever be grateful to you for telling me the things I didn't want to hear.

In 2006, I had the good fortune of meeting Keith Woodward. Keith taught me how to ride a bike. He comforted me when my leg was broken and promised me I would race again. For over ten years, I have been calling him and asking, "Do you think I can do this?" His answer remains the same, "I know you can." Keith, you have made my dreams your dreams. Your friendship and unwavering support mean the world to me.

To Andrew Shanks, who took me on as an overexcited athlete and was my first real multi-sport coach. You introduced me to structure, capturing data, and most importantly, to listening to someone else.

While Jason was racing Epicman I was fortunate enough to meet his friend, Kellie Smirnoff. She was the lone female participant in the event. It was the first time I ever saw a race with just one woman in it. Thank you for the confidence you instilled in me and for continuing to encourage me to go bigger.

To Heather Jones-Proctor who coached me through Race Across America. You didn't bat an eyelash when I told you what we wanted to do. You're one of the most enthusiastic people I have ever had the pleasure of meeting. Thank you for believing in me.

I have spent countless hours with too many extraordinary athletes over the years to list them all here. I want to thank everyone who has spent time training with me and offering me words of support and encouragement. To my Dynamo Multisport family, a.k.a. *dynamafia*, you guys are simply the best team out there.

To the lifeguards at Dynamo pool who opened doors early for me or allowed me to stay a little late to get in my gazllionth meter, thank you. You might not have understood my craziness, but you certainly supported it.

To Kyle Pease and the incredible athletes and volunteers who make the Kyle Pease Foundation possible, thank you. Thank you for showing me what it means to shatter limitations and to race with heart. Thank you for allowing me the opportunity to give back to the community I love so much by racing with your athletes.

I am grateful for my best friend of over 20 years, Karen Ewing, for her brutal honesty and constant friendship. You have zero interest in triathlons or ultras, yet you have never tried to persuade me to give up something that you know brings me such happiness.

I've been fortunate to have some remarkably strong women in my life as mentors and role models. When I began my journey to a life of health I worked for two amazing women, Libba and Martha, who supported me wholeheartedly. As the years have passed, my role in the organization has changed a lot, and my personal goals and achievements have as well. One thing has remained the same, and that is working in an environment that appreciates and supports strong women.

To Eileen Steil, my friend and massage therapist. I am forever indebted to you for the hours you have spent working on my body. You very graciously shared your ultra-racing wisdom with me, warning me yet still encouraging me. Thank you for making me feel normal while taking on not-so-normal things.

To Maria Thrash, thank you for your dedication to turning me into a swimmer. You pushed the limits of what I thought was possible and kept it fun. You are one of the most resilient athletes I know and will always remain one of my favorite people to get dropped by on a ride.

Ultra-racing would not be possible without people willing to volunteer their time as crew. I've had the great fortune of meeting some of the most selfless people known to Earth over the years who have volunteered their time and energy to help me cross finish lines safely. To Chuck Mathison, Keith Woodward, Jill Poon, Emily Beaulieu, George Darden, Kim Stumpf, Anne Lovett, Will Dillard, Ben Murphy, Leslie Shapiro, Beau Bearden, Stephen Overbaugh, Hilary Murdock, and Jason Overbaugh, thank you from the bottom of my heart for your sacrifices.

Epic 5 was a unique and beautiful experience that is made possible by group of people who embody the spirit of what ultra-racing should be. Thank you to Jason Lester for creating the event and Rebecca Morgan for your steadfast leadership during the event. You are the kind of person I want to be stuck in a foxhole with. Many mahalos to the event staff and local volunteers, Scott, Jen, Mary Margaret, Colin, Mike, Victoria, Kim, Chet, Jen #2, Wil, Adam, Jodi, Todd, Lyndsey, and Amy who made becoming the first female to finish Epic 5 possible.

To Hilary Murdock, who enthusiastically said she wanted to be a part of Epic 5 the moment she found out about it. I can never repay you for the energy you put into me. You managed to do it all with a smile on your face and never uttered even the faintest of complaints. Thank you for your support and most importantly for being my friend.

To Brent Pease, my coach, mentor and friend: thank you for your relentless pursuit of all things amazing. Thank you for your devotion to excellence and passion for the sport and your athletes. Without your guidance and reassurance, Epic 5 would not have been possible.

I consider myself very fortunate to have two parents who are complete opposites. They are unique in their own ways and have taught me to be the person that I am today. To my mom, thank you for teaching me early on that normal was boring, its okay to jump out of airplanes and off cliffs, and that life was meant to live. To my dad, thank you for making me tough as nails, being my model and my hero. Not a day goes by that I don't think about how much I love you.

Most of all, I want to thank the love of my life, Jason, for loving me as the imperfect and different person that I am. Never once have you wavered in your support of me. You have pushed me past my limits and taught me how to be comfortable being uncomfortable. You give me the courage and strength I need to make these awesome adventures possible. When I have been broken and gutted to my shell, you put me back together and made me press forward. Your work ethic and drive to succeed make me a better person. Sharing life with you is the most beautiful journey I have ever taken.

I would like to thank each and every person who has taken the time to encourage me to share my story. I am touched by the people who have reached out to me over the years and told me that this journey has given them hope that change is possible. I wrote this book in hopes of showing others that might be struggling that you are much stronger than you think and capable of amazing things. May your journey be filled with gratitude for this gift of life.

THE UNPLEASANT TRUTH

*Even the most daring and accomplished people have
undergone tremendous difficulty. In fact, the more successful
they became, the more they attributed their success to the
lessons learned from their most difficult times. Adversity is
our teacher. When we view adversity as a guide towards
greater inner growth, we will then learn to accept the wisdom
our soul came into this life to learn.*

—Barbara Rose

There's an old African proverb that says, "A lie has many variations, the truth none." True to that adage, my moment of absolute truth took place during my annual physical in November of 2004. I was only 23 years old. I had been a faithful patient of Dr. Davidson for quite a few years, and though almost no one goes to a doctor just for fun, this visit turned out to be one that changed my life.

In his late seventies, Dr. Warren Davidson was a slim man with a slight build and beautiful silver hair. Picture the super-wise ancient wizard guy from the Harry Potter movie, now take away his magic scepter and replace it with a stethoscope, lose the beard, and add some ear hair. I prefer that people (especially people with something important to say…for example, doctors) speak directly and not try to sugarcoat a message—it seems like a lot of time gets wasted and points get missed by diluting the message with warm and fuzzy talk. Dr. Davidson was fairly well known for being direct, so we were simpatico in that respect. Though small in physical stature, he was not gentle by any means; if you needed to hear something for your own good, he would tell you quite clearly. That is not to say he didn't care for his patients; in fact I always felt like he cared deeply and genuinely about my well-being.

Dr. Davidson went through his typical regimen of poking, prodding, writing things down, reflecting, listening, measuring, testing, and making the occasional grunt that indicated that he was thinking about *doctory* stuff. Everything seemed to be going along splendidly, and I anticipated him signing off with a *"see you next year"* and rambling on to his next patient. As our visit came to an end, he sat at his desk, pulled his glasses to the tip of his nose, and slowly thumbed through my medical file. Then he started doing things you don't want your doctor to do. He brought his hand to his mouth, thoughtfully removed and replaced his glasses, slowly rubbed his chin, and nodded his head with unease. I'm sitting on the edge of an exam table wearing a super fashionable paper shirt, feeling even more self-conscious than I should have at the moment. I had a suspicion that I was about to hear something I probably wouldn't enjoy. *Isn't it funny how we want to run and hide, even as adults, when we know we are about to get bad news, even though we know it will change absolutely nothing? In fact, not hearing it will probably only make things worse.* So I did what any grown woman would do—I stuck my fingers in my ears and went *LALALALALALA*. Just kidding, I took it like a big girl.

After the very definition of a deafening silence for what seemed like six hours, he said, "Ms. Grabol, do you realize that you have gained 17 pounds since you saw me just last year?" I could feel my face instantly warm with embarrassment as I swallowed a heaping helping of cold hard fact with a side of whipped humiliation. "Oh, have I?" I asked sheepishly. I knew I had gained some weight, but honestly had no idea how much. My clothes had become tighter and been replaced by larger clothes, and my scale had somehow vanished from my bathroom because it, like Dr. Davidson, was telling me a bunch of stuff I didn't want to hear.

Just in case I wasn't fully comprehending what he was telling me, he put it in the context of more facts and historical trends. Dr. Davidson continued spraying statistics at me like some kind of truth sprinkler: "And the year before that, you gained almost 15 pounds." I gulped and remained silent, feeling my skin burn as I hung my head in shame. "I see from your history that all four of your grandparents died from heart attacks. Is that correct?" I swallowed hard and muttered under my breath, "Yes, that's correct." *Now if you'll excuse me, I have a box of oatmeal raisin cookies I would like to get back to.*

I fidgeted, uncomfortably waiting for the doctor's painful line of questioning to stop, feeling a bit more like I was seated on a witness stand than on the examination table. "At this rate you will likely weigh 300 pounds by the time you are 30, you will be a diabetic by age 40, and will not even live to see 50. You are a beautiful young lady, but you should really take better care of yourself. *Three hundred pounds. At thirty years old.* The thought actually gave me chills. That's reality show territory—and not the good kind.

My heart rate went up as if to foreshadow what would be the next decade of my life. I waited for him to stop and just write me some type of prescription or at least leave me with instructions on how to manage my out-of-control weight gain via the miracle of modern medicine. If Dr. Davidson had a miracle cure, he wasn't sharing it with me. He knew that my condition could only be blamed on one thing, and that was *me*. Further, he knew the disservice he would be doing me by trying to cushion the blow. My life may very well depend on my receiving this message. Dr. Davidson stood up, shook my hand, and left the room, closing the door firmly behind him. Another throwback to childhood was my almost immediate and overwhelming desire to hurl every excuse in the world at him for my increase in weight and decrease in overall health. In retrospect, this was one of the most uncomfortable yet wonderful conversations of my life.

I was a grown-up, and this was my problem and mine alone. I was looking at my own mortality for the first time in my life and being forced to make a choice. I just wanted to cry. I had been called out by a doctor whom I knew and trusted, and the truth was about as easy to swallow as a tablespoon of cinnamon. Seriously. You can't swallow that. Don't try it. Okay, try it, but don't blame me when the rest of your day is ruined because you tried something stupid.

I tore the hospital gown off my back, rolled it into a ball, and threw it into the trash as if it were to blame. As I changed back into my oversized sweatshirt, I did something that I had stopped doing a long time ago (for the same reason my bathroom scale was now under a potted plant and I was wearing super boxy oversized clothes). I took a long, slow gaze at myself in the full-length mirror. I didn't even recognize the 220-pound woman looking sheepishly back at me. The truth was that, prior to my 15 minutes of shame with Dr. Davidson, I really and truly had no idea how much I weighed. I knew the general trend of things wasn't what experts would call *positive*, but I had just resigned myself to letting it happen, thinking I would somehow miraculously wake up thin one day. At 23, most people are generally healthy, but I felt lethargic, frumpy, awkward, and incredibly unattractive. My once flourishing self-esteem had also suffered, getting lower with every pound I gained. I felt like I didn't even know the person mocking my reflection as I slumped away. It was time for a change.

KNOW THINE ENEMY

I figured if I'm going to fix this, I needed to identify the problems, habits, and patterns at the center of it all and how this was changing me. My doctor had been honest enough to start me down this path, so now it was time to look at every aspect of my life and identify exactly how it is working for or against me. This meant everything from the obvious diet and exercise to hobbies, my job, figuring out how much my genetics will allow me, and even examining my personal relationships. I figured I had my youth (which comes with an astounding ability to bounce back from even huge mistakes, because that is when you make most of them), my family, and a good network of friends working in my favor. That is a lot more than many people have, so I'm a long way from the finish line, but I am off to a decent start. Now to the unpleasant business of dissecting what my life really consists of...

Shopping is a pastime most young women love, but when you have to scour the racks for something that could pass as stylish in the plus-size section, and shop in places that have the word "barn" in their title, it isn't as fun as it was in my teenage years. I dressed like...well, it wasn't really *dressing*, as much as *disguising myself*. I wore clothes that would strategically hide my shape and cover as much of me as possible. I was very realistic about what my body looked like, although I felt as though I carried my weight really well. I was extremely bottom heavy, so it was easy for me to conceal my actual size. I had become an expert on what to wear and what not to even attempt.

I would not describe myself as being particularly talented athletically as a child. I grew up mostly taking dance classes (though never to be mistaken for anything resembling a dancer). My height made me a natural choice for basketball, but that was short lived when my coach realized I was only good at rebounding and fouling out, which I later learned aren't actual positions on the court. As I got older, I tried my hand at cheerleading (more a *base of the pyramid* kind of gal than a *hey, let's throw you a million feet in the air and then try to catch you* type). I enjoyed softball in my teenage years, although, looking back, I think I enjoyed going to the ballpark and ordering Frito Pies more than actually playing. Though I tried hard and enjoyed being involved, I was not a natural athlete. Reaching almost 5'8" before my 13th birthday meant I was almost always the tallest and largest person on any team or group of other girls my age. Instead of being tall and slender, I was tall and curvaceous. I believe "Rubenesque" is the euphemism of the day…although aptly named after a sandwich…or maybe an artist. *Who is named after a sandwich?* I learned early on that I was not the girl who could eat whatever she wanted without affecting how I filled out my uniforms or dance leotards. I was forever the tallest person in my class until the boys finally hit puberty.

My earliest realization of my large frame occurred in 1985 at an Olan Mills family photography studio. I was dolled up in the most stunning purple dress with white lace gloves that ended just above my wrist. As I began to strike a pose, the photographer pointed at my stomach and told me to *suck it in.* At the age of four, I had no idea what he meant, but gathered from the way he was poking my doughy stomach that whatever I was doing wasn't very becoming. I still have the picture to this day, and every time I look at it, I feel myself subconsciously sucking in. That one comment led me to develop some type of *posed photo phobia,* which I never recovered from.

My lack of real athleticism is sort of a family trait, although I do remember my dad doing push-ups and sit-ups every day. As a former Marine, he enjoyed a certain level of regimented activity. My dad is very tall and slender. My mother and I have completely opposite frames, as she is extremely petite with ivory skin and red hair. Though never athletic, Mom was always hyperconscious of her appearance (likely a result of being so attractive), and I struggled to develop a positive self-image that was not directly related to my appearance. Mom was on a perpetual diet, ranging from cabbage soup to Atkins to Weight Watchers to whatever Diet *du jour* was in vogue at the time. She would constantly be participating in jazzercise classes and would spend countless hours in front of the TV exercising to workout videos. Like most teenage girls, I spent a considerable amount of time dieting, thinking about dieting, preparing to diet, or finishing a diet. How big I looked in something was at the forefront of my mind every day while dressing. I distinctly remember in 1997, when the FDA banned the popular diet drug fen-phen, because I knew so many outraged women who were taking it. *I know it makes your heart leak and can kill you, but I'm trying to get skinny without doing any work, okay?!*

I mentally traced back my steps to how I ballooned to 220 pounds. I ate like a typical teenager all through high school, meaning I basically ate like a stoned raccoon. Like most kids my age, burgers, fries, and pizza were the staples of my diet. I was very conscious of my body and fearful of becoming overweight. It was never really *cool* to eat much lunch in school, and I remember eating as little as possible most days for lunch. Diet Coke and celery, of all things, made up the bulk of my lunchtime menu! When not on display in the cafeteria, I gorged on fast food. Playing sports and maintaining a moderate level of activity kept me from becoming overweight as a teenager.

It's hard for me to determine exactly *why* I was eating the way I was. Growing up, my mother placed a high value on aesthetics, and as a nurse she was very aware of her health. As a single parent, she didn't have time to cook much, so we ate a variety of foods that were convenient and simple. As my brother and I reached our teenage years, we started eating a lot more junk food. I was never a picky eater, so finding things I liked to eat was never an issue. My diet consisted primarily of four major food groups: McDonald's, Chick-Fil-A, Chinese take-out, and pizza. Fruits and vegetables were nonexistent in my diet (unless you count the pickle on my Big Mac as a cucumber, and oh yeah, ketchup is a vegetable, right?). I ate at the Golden Arches four to five times per week, and naturally I super-sized everything I ordered, because they asked…and you know…I didn't want to be rude.

Once I graduated high school, my activity came to a screeching halt. Not subjected to eating in a cafeteria of judgmental teenagers meant I could eat whatever I wanted, whenever I wanted. And eat is exactly what I did. My eating habits went from moderately bad to borderline offensive and possibly illegal. I thought about food all around the clock—the saltier the better. The ideal day in college would be one in which I would eat a Chick-Fil-A chicken biscuit and hash browns for breakfast, with coffee (loaded with cream and sugar); a McDonald's Quarter Pounder with cheese meal (value sized with a coke to drink, of course) for lunch; and chicken lo mein for dinner. I loved fried foods, Mexican, and Chinese take-out. The frosting on the cake, so to speak, were the weekends routinely spent overindulging in alcohol. Though I had quit smoking regularly when I was 21, I always smoked when I drank. I should have had a team of scientists following me around to see just how quickly one's lifestyle can end one's life. My weight increased steadily. I had gained the famous *Freshman Fifteen* during my first year of college at Georgia State University and then proceeded to the *Sophomore Seventeen*, the *Junior Nineteen*, and the *Senior Sweet Lord What The Hell Happened?* I don't know exactly how much weight I gained during that era, but I ballooned from a size 8 to a size 16–18; five sizes in less than five years.

It was very eye opening to me to discover what a role my job played, because all you ever hear about is diet and exercise when it comes to being healthy. Add up all of the time a normal person spends eating and exercising in a day, and you probably have less than two hours. Now consider the six to nine hours you spend at work and how that may be hindering your progress. It is a bit mind numbing. I started working a nine-to-five job and my eating habits got even worse. My day would normally start with several large cups of coffee-flavored sugar (seriously, my sugar/cream/coffee proportions were obscene to the point that everyone joked about it). As the day wore on, things would get progressively worse. I usually didn't actually eat food until about ten o'clock, and by that point I was so hungry I would eat just about anything to last me until lunch. And I'm not talking about a handful of raw almonds, unless they were coated in nougat and dipped in chocolate. Lunch usually consisted of Chinese or fried chicken take-out, followed by more eating out or ordering pizza to take home for dinner. On the rare occasion that I did fire up the stove and actually cook, it was often a heavy casserole, macaroni and cheese, or sausage cheese balls. My drink of choice was sweet tea, and growing up in Georgia, sweet tea is S-W-E-E-T. I prepared mine with a full cup of sugar per pitcher. Knowing what I know now about nutrition, I'd imagine my internal organs and the chemistry in my body were just chaos. I mean like nine cats tied to each other in a refrigerator box and someone turns on a vacuum cleaner chaos. The human body is truly amazing and, thankfully, very forgiving.

I found myself exiting Dr. Davidson's office feeling pretty much the same as I felt leaving the jerkball photographer at Olan Mills nearly 20 years earlier. Over the years, I had learned exactly what it meant to suck in, and now I also had to suck it up and rebound from what I now knew as the truth. I was uncomfortable in my skin, and my body felt foreign to me most days. Chronologically, I was only 23, but physically, I felt three times my age. As I drove home from my appointment, I obsessed about my family history. My paternal grandfather died in his thirties from a massive heart attack. My paternal grandmother died at only 42. I couldn't deny that genetics were not in my favor. I never expected that at age 23 I might be literally approaching the halfway point of my life.

It was a long drive home. What the doctor said was absolutely true, and no amount of rationalizing or excuse making could get me out of this. I was overweight, and I was lazy. I felt awful and looked equally awful. I wasn't sure if this was rock bottom, but I could certainly see it from where I stood. I was dating a really sweet guy, named Casey, but knew we wouldn't spend the rest of our lives together. He never complained about my size, although in our four years together, I had gained a tremendous amount of weight. I had also developed a really bad relationship with food. I ate when I was sad. I ate when I was happy. I ate when I was bored. I had been in denial about what the excessive eating had done to my body by avoiding the scale and steering clear of mirrors whenever possible. *If you can't see it, it doesn't exist* was my internal philosophy. In many ways, I was the emperor parading the streets in my new clothes, only mine were severely ill fitting and large. Dr. Davidson gave me the facts, and I had to make a decision. Was I ready to have a possibly life-threatening medical event before my mid twenties, or was I ready to make a change? Well, jeez, when you put it that way, the answer sounds pretty simple. It was one hell of a day.

That night for dinner, I did what most people do when they are *going to start a diet tomorrow*. I ate like there was no tomorrow. I ordered a pizza and a bucket of wings and ate until I was literally about to pop. My stomach felt so full. I dipped my pizza in ranch dressing and thought, *this is so frickin' good*, except it really wasn't. The normal warm, familiar feeling I usually got when I gorged out on a favorite meal wasn't there anymore. This was the event horizon. I was finally ready to change.

PICK APART THINE ENEMY

As we all know, change isn't easy. Over the years, I have changed that saying to—*nothing easy is worth having*—because if it was easy, everyone would do it, and it would thus have no worth. The difficulty in changing your lifestyle to the extent that I needed to change mine could easily be compounded if my friends, family, and coworkers were not on board. I was fortunate enough to have grown up with some basic knowledge of what was healthy versus what was not. For some people, learning the basics of nutrition is the first step to cleaning up their eating. After all, we can't change what we don't realize we are doing incorrectly, right? I made a laundry list of all the things I needed to change, and it read like *War and Peace*. Basically, everything I did involving my diet was bad; I skipped meals, snacked, cooked with tons of salt (if I even cooked), and ate portions large enough for two people. Basically, it came down to this: healthy people exercised as much as I ate, and ate about as much as I exercised. I probably ate more than I exercised, as I did not exercise, but it sounds better the other way.

I decided it would be easier if I broke my eating habits down to weekly changes. The first week, I gave up using sugar and creamer in my coffee. I swapped it out for a natural sweetener and nonfat creamer, which tasted like some kind of industrial solvent and left me hungry. Since 500 calories worth of morning coffee was no longer to be part of my day, I decided it was time to begin eating breakfast. I knew someone who drank smoothies, and they seemed all lithe and shiny and healthy, so smoothies seemed like a good idea for me, too. I played around with the combinations of fruits and veggies for a couple of weeks and started looking up recipes for different ways to blend up a breakfast that I could tolerate. My body's rejection of this new regimen literally started at my teeth—they were sensitive to the cold and would become enmeshed with stupid berry seeds, which wasn't a great look. There were many times when the idea of cleaning out the blender seemed a Sisyphean task. On the other hand, I couldn't deny that the smoothie made me feel so much better than a sausage, egg, and cheese biscuit. I needed to stick with it. Soon enough, I was the smoothie queen and loved my early morning dose of energy!

Lunch and dinner were harder. I had never prepared much food for myself. My mom didn't cook very often when I was growing up, so I was accustomed to eating mostly frozen meals. As an adult, I continued eating them, and they were not very healthy. I started paying attention to the calories in my meals for the first time ever and picked up Lean Cuisine and Weight Watchers meals instead of Stouffers. I was a novice in the kitchen but decided that I needed to start cooking. The only cook-book I had owned up until this point in my life was titled *The Four Ingredient Cookbook,* which included recipes for such favorites as cocktail sausage balls. It is difficult to screw up a recipe that has only four ingredients.

I realized that in order to control exactly what I was eating, I would need to prepare more of it myself, so I bought some legitimate cook-books and tried to learn as much as I could about cooking healthy foods. I was introduced to the novel idea that a vegetable *can* actually be the main part of your meal (who knew?), and the notion that not all meats needed to be breaded and fried. I was changing the way I was eating, and the results were noticeable almost immediately. Fruits and vegetables became a staple in my daily eating. Rather than eating three square meals a day, I started to eat smaller meals more frequently. I cut out the sugary desserts and started to taste foods before I would dump salt all over them. In addition to making better decisions around what foods I put into my body, I started to practice self-control, a phrase I had heard uttered by others but with which I was not personally familiar. I could finally be around tempting foods without feeling the excruciatingly overwhelming desire to try everything. I stuck to the plan even when it was tough. I started practicing portion control and not eating the entire meal when I went out to eat. I paid attention to food labels and did research on what different types of fats were. I started reading about ways to make healthy meals that actually tasted palatable. My friends laughed at me because, wherever I would go, I would always have food in my purse. Yet who do you think they came to when they needed a snack?

I learned that if I always had a good choice that was readily available to me, it would significantly decrease my chances of making bad choices. My friends were still not completely understanding or accepting of my newfound desire to lose weight and eat healthier. I found myself sometimes frustrated by people who said things like, *come on, just have one slice of pizza—it won't kill you,* and, *I know it's healthy, but doesn't eating like that just make you want to kill yourself?*, and, *I'd do the same thing but I JUST LOVE DOUGHNUTS!* I wanted to say, *yes, doing the right thing can be challenging and, yes, we all like some stuff that isn't good for us. But I am discovering a certain mastery of myself that just might be the most powerful part of me.*

My body was responding as any organism would if you stopped poisoning it and instead gave it the things it needed. I felt far more energetic. My problem skin was starting to clear up. It was so much easier to stay on track when I was able to associate the positive changes I was experiencing directly with how my body felt. My clothes kept getting looser and looser. People were noticing that I was losing weight and began giving me positive feedback about my appearance. Did I ever feel like I was depriving myself? Of course. Refer to the statement earlier in the chapter about worthwhile things not being easy, if you need clarity on that. I grew up with an Italian father, so our entire lives were built around food—what we will eat, when we will eat it, what it will taste like. It was really hard to go out with friends and know that I was the one ordering tap water and a single grape (not really, but sometimes it felt that way) while they were diving face first into a plate of nachos delbeefo that could fill a pillowcase. While I felt deprived at times, I knew that the reason I had gained all the weight in the first place was because I *never* deprived myself of anything. I rewarded myself for every action, both positive and negative, with my best friend in the whole world—food. Years of not practicing any self-control were what got me into this mess to begin with. I was working hard to make sure that I didn't slip back into those old habits.

At some point, the people in my office began following my lead and began to eat a little healthier, too. Suddenly we all stopped ordering out, and the refrigerator was full of our Tupperware containers. Just like the bad habits that rubbed off on each other, our good habits seemed to be spreading, too. We always had a large bowl of junk food snacks that we replenished for all staff to stoke their sugar high. The bowl started staying full for longer and longer until we reached the point where we rarely touched it.

When I could walk up a flight of stairs without being out of breath, I decided that it was time to try working out. I was losing weight, but it wasn't coming off nearly as quickly as I had put it on. One night, I was looking down at my legs and noticed they were much slimmer than they had always been but lacked any type of definition or strength. I remember commenting on it to Casey, who was far too sweet. He told me I was perfect the way I was. He was so kind and caring, but also totally complacent with everything in our lives, and complacent wasn't part of how I wanted to move forward. We were starting to drift farther and farther apart. I was setting goals for myself and felt like he was indifferent one way or the other. He was never negative or unsupportive in any way; he just never cared (or at least he never told me that he cared) what size I was. I certainly appreciated our relationship together and the fact that he had never pointed out all the weight I had gained. I was also starting to feel like our lives were maturing and we were going in two totally separate directions.

I *wanted* to work out, but the problem was that I didn't know anyone who went to the gym. I literally had zero friends who worked out. I knew that walking was healthy and inexpensive, so I figured I would start there. I joined Mom a few times for walks around a local park. My energy levels were increasing, and I felt like I could do more. The idea of joining a gym seemed really intimidating when, only a month earlier, I was circling parking lots looking for the closest possible parking spot. I have a cousin, Kathy, who has a video that she created called *Piloga*. It is a Pilates/yoga fusion. I thought *Yogates* sounded better, but I'm not in the exercise video naming business. I popped the DVD in to give it a try. Ten minutes into it, I was *confausted.* That's confused and exhausted. I'm basically just trying to get my stretch on, and I'm sweating like a German trying to tell a joke? I was barely even moving! Kathy kept telling me to breathe and focus on my core. At the time, I wasn't sure where my core was, but I knew for a fact that it was malfunctioning and on fire.

I wasn't really used to trying things that were physically difficult at this point in my life. The sports I had played growing up were not incredibly competitive, and I was not a high-level athlete by any means. This was the first time as an adult I was making an attempt to be a healthier person, and it was really, *really* challenging. I assumed that all I had to do was eat some vegetables, and I would be back to my high school size. I didn't realize how hard losing weight would be, especially considering how easy it was to gain it. I was being forced to make choices on a daily basis and continue to follow through with the commitment I had made to myself. I had no one who was holding me accountable for my actions. It was turning out to be an incredibly personal and enlightening exercise—nobody would know or care if I *shame ate* an entire pizza naked in my bathroom. That was completely for me to decide to do or not to do, as the consequences were completely mine as well.

This was a pivotal point for me in my journey. It was not easy. Casey and I had a very amicable breakup after four years of dating. My mother was getting remarried soon. I felt anxious about being in her wedding in front of our family. Cooking was hard, and being prepared with food was hard. Turning down things I loved to eat was really hard. Going to restaurants and not eating what your friends ate wasn't much fun, either. Now I was trying to work out, and that was hard, too. I was starting to wonder if any of it would ever be easy or at least fun. It was rewarding so far, but it got a bit dark to think that I might always miss those foods, and it might always hurt to exercise. But there was only one way to find out, and I knew the alternative course all too well.

If there's one thing I hate, it's not excelling at things. The only thing worse than not excelling is not being able to do something at all. Being that out of shape physically was a huge blow to my ego. I wasn't even 25, and there were people twice my age on that Piloga video running circles around me. This made me angry and motivated. Once that fire was lit inside me, there was no turning back. I did the video so many times that I could do it with my eyes closed, repeating every word my cousin Kathy said. Eventually, I felt that I was coordinated and flexible, and for the first time I could remember, I felt like I had the confidence to exercise in public.

I went for walks. I climbed up a local hiking trail, but I found everything to be rather boring and lacking stimulation. I decided it was time to try throwing some weights around, so I joined the local gym. The gym was much more than I was prepared for. There was shiny equipment and weights, plus every cardio machine possible. I figured out pretty quickly that cardio was harder than I thought it would be. Instead of admitting I had no endurance, I would just do 15 minutes of each machine for variety. The truth was that, at the 14:59 mark, I was ready to get off and take a break and sometimes wanted to find the inventor of said machine to see if there was any chance he or she could be convicted of some kind of crime against humanity. But I'd take my break and climb onto the next contraption to give it a go.

By May of 2005, I had lost close to 70 pounds. I had a pair of jeans I had bought several years earlier that wouldn't even fit over my knees when I started all of this madness. The first time I got them on, zipped up, and realized they were LOOSE, I literally cried. I still own those jeans, more than ten years later, as a reminder of what I had accomplished. I loved running into people who I had not seen in a while and having them notice my transformation. Shopping was no longer something I dreaded because nothing would fit me. My joints didn't ache when I walked. I could manage to carry groceries into my house without being out of breath. I was gaining confidence in my appearance. This was what it was all about and why it felt so good to have endured the times when I had doubts. This was worthwhile, not easy. This wasn't always fun, but always satisfying.

By the summer of that year, I was a full-fledged gym rat. Everyone there knew me. I loved pushing myself. I was stronger than the average woman and loved knowing I could open a jar of peanut butter without asking for help. I should have been satisfied with my progress to that point, but I wasn't. The truth was that I still found the gym to be kind of boring. As much as I tried to vary my routines, I was still in a big air-conditioned box lifting weights. I pored over *Shape* and *Women's Health* magazines looking for the next big thing, but I never really discovered it. I finally had a lot of energy, and working out was the way that I controlled my energy. I had always struggled to fall asleep at night and found that sleep came easily to me after I would exhaust myself in the gym every evening.

I figured I had pretty much tried everything the gym had to offer except for one thing…spin class. The spin room was this tiny, dimly lit room that blasted heart-pumping music. It had a mystery about it, like the gym was for people who stayed fit, but in there…that's where the *athletes* were. People went into that room looking relatively normal (as normal as one can look in padded spandex) and came out looking like they had been fighting for their lives. They looked totally spent, with smiles on their faces. I managed to get my roommate at the time to join the gym, and eventually she agreed to take a spin class with me. We fumbled around with the bike seats trying to adjust it to the least painful position. The thoughts that go through your head at your first spin class are usually, *Oh dear Lord, my nether regions. This is so painful. Does anyone else smell smoke? At some point my heart has to either stop or leave my body. Why am I here?* The discomfort of the saddle was a nice distraction from the fact that my heart rate was close to 170 and I couldn't breathe. I left my first class looking as if I had wrestled a bear. My butt hurt, my legs hurt, I was exhausted and thirsty, yet very satisfied. I loved it.

It didn't take long for me to figure out that you could take two classes back to back, buy a gel saddle cover for the bike seat and special spandex shorts with padding built in, all of which cut down on injury and irritation in and around the "danger zone." I was in the saddle and riding high.

People often ask me how you resist tempting foods when you are trying to lose weight or eat healthier. The truth is that you cannot always resist the temptations that are around you. What you can do is think about your day and your week as a series of choices around what foods you will put into your body. Aim to make 80 percent of those choices healthy foods. If you deny yourself the occasional pizza or ice cream, you might find that you begin to resent your diet for being too rigid. Instead of focusing on what you *can't* or *shouldn't* have, try focusing your attention on the positive feelings that you associate with eating healthy, or seeing a new weight on the scale. Set small incremental goals along the way to your end goal, and reward yourself as you make them. Personally, buying a new outfit was an excellent reward for me, and I don't even like shopping! I would even buy things that didn't quite fit right, knowing that once I met my next goal they would fit perfectly!

When you mess up (notice I said *when* and not *if*, because you are not perfect, and you will make mistakes!) and eat two pieces of cake for breakfast just remember...you have the remainder of the day to make better choices for yourself. Some people think, *well, I already screwed up breakfast; I might as well eat this cheeseburger for lunch.* This mentality will never get you to your goals! If you got off the highway at the wrong exit, would you stop and build a house or would you get back on the highway headed in the right direction?

The more wrong turns you make, the longer your trip will take, but I promise you that if you continue the course, you will end up where you want to be!

2

GYM RAT TO TRIATHLETE

Ability is what you are capable of doing. Motivation determines what you do. Attitude determines how well you do it.

—Lou Holtz

I was at the gym one evening with my roommate when I noticed a group of people in the aerobics room working out. There were eight of them, and they had the most bizarre setup for an aerobics class that I had ever seen. After continuing to stare at them like some kind of creep, I realized they weren't doing an aerobics class at all. They had steps lined up against the wall and another step on the floor. They would hop up on the box, then do step-ups, followed by lateral jumps over the step. Then they bunny-hopped across the room and did walking lunges to return. As if this weren't enough, they would complete their routine by holding plank for a minute. The music was blasting, and they looked focused on their mission, but at the same time they were clearly having fun. They appeared to be athletic, but the kind of "athletic" that looks natural and healthy—like humans were supposed to look when we spent our days looking for food and fighting off animals instead of reading Facebook and eating out of Styrofoam contain-ers. Who *were* these beautiful nerds, and what were they doing?

Upon some further investigation, I learned that these weirdos were a local group of triathletes. As I gazed at them in total and complete awe, I told my roommate, "I wish my arms looked like hers." She responded, in a matter of fact way, "They do."

That was good to hear, but I wanted my strength to have utility. It felt good to be as fit as I was, but essentially I was good at lifting weights and a few other things in a prescribed way. What these people were doing was helping them become much more athletically well rounded, and I guessed that would translate well to everyday life...and fighting off the occasional wildcat, should that ever come up.

One evening, I ended up taking a spin class taught by one of them, and we struck up a conversation about riding. I actually owned a road bike that I had bought shortly after I started my journey to lose weight in hopes of doing a triathlon. I had gone on a ride with a friend of mine, Victor. Not long after the ride, his older brother was struck by a car while on a training ride and passed away. The incident shook me up so much that I put the bike away and had not touched it since. I didn't know much about riding, much less riding safely, nor did I have many resources to pull from. Now I had people I could potentially ride with and, more importantly, learn from. *Was this the answer to my boring gym routine?* I wasn't happy with just showing up and doing workouts anymore. The gym had served its purpose, but I needed a goal bigger than hitting numbers on a scale. Something was missing; something more challenging. I suspected that triathlon was my answer.

I was happy to learn that these triathletes were far less intimidating than I anticipated. Keith, Dana, Joe, Vanessa, and Kelly were kind enough to invite me to a bike ride at a local park called Stone Mountain. Cleverly named, the park's main feature is a large mountain made entirely of beaver pelts. Just kidding, it's stone. It's really a pretty park—lots of trees, water, many places to hike and run and ride, and very recreation friendly.

I showed up for the ride wearing what I thought would be acceptable clothing. I need to give kudos to the group I was riding with—they were all dressed like they were going into space and riding bikes that weighed less than my tennis shoes and completely disappeared if you looked at them head-on, yet nobody even hinted at judging me. I learned over the years that triathlon is extremely humbling and, despite the fact that a triathlete has never been spotted in the wild not wearing some kind of triathlon-related clothing, they all remember very well how hard it once was (and sometimes still is). I don't guess I expected them refuse to ride with me, but I was clearly a cub among lions. My loose-fitting shirt didn't match my shorts, and I couldn't help but notice how uncoordinated I appeared to be compared to everyone else. We rode a couple five-mile loops around the mountain. My tennis shoes and toe cages were bulky and large compared to the groups' carbon fiber titanium shoe/pedal combinations. I knew that I would immediately plummet face first into the pavement if I took even one hand off the handlebars, so I opted to leave my water bottle safely in its little cage.

By the third loop, I was getting pretty thirsty, so I reluctantly took my hand off the bike to reach down and grab my water bottle from the cage; that instantly sent it skittering down the road. By now, the group had tired of waiting on me. My friend, Keith, was kind enough to stop and retrieve my bottle for me, and we caught up with the group as they waited for us at a stop sign. There is a saying that goes, "We are being educated when we know it least." Right now I was taking a class called, "Nutrition 101—Bad things happen when you try to burn fuel you don't have." I was obviously fading fast. Nutrition and hydration are critical, even on rides that are *only* 18 miles long. Someone offered me a little packet of something called a *gel*. Like the name implied, it was a slimy, oozing product with honey-like consistency. As I was about to open it, someone offered the helpful tip, "Sometimes those give people diarrhea." Oh, the conundrum. *Am I hungry enough to risk never seeing these people again?* Not quite that hungry. Yet.

A while later, we were approaching a total ride mileage of 18 miles. This seemed like a really, *really* long ride. *Surely this is the part of the day when we all break for brunch, right?* Nope. Turns out the triathletes were just getting warmed up. They would ride a couple more loops and then do a two-mile run. "Did I want to join?" they asked. "Gee, guys, I'd really love to, but it seems that someone has removed the bones and muscles from my legs and replaced them with wet sand and agony. So no, I won't be running right now."

Since we all worked out at the same gym, the local group let me join them for their swim workouts as well. I thought that I *knew how to swim*. What I really knew was *how not to drown*. It turns out there is a major difference that involves timing, efficiency, body position, and coordination...all of which I had left in my other purse. A really kind guy named Bill, who also raced triathlons and swam in college, was helping everyone with their swim strokes. I was easily the least talented of the group. Bill took pity on my terrible form and gave me endless pointers. To this day, I still think about him telling me to *keep my elbows bent* and *scoop the water like a bowl of cereal*, and *stop screaming obscenities when you breathe*. Swimming was so exhausting that I would almost always come home ready to devour everything in sight. I hearkened back to the bad old days when I would do that for no reason at all.

I had absolutely no concept of structured training for an event, so I just followed the group around and tagged along to their workouts. The fact that half of them were training for an *Ironman* meant nothing to me. Did I even realize what an *Ironman* was? Something that really fit and perhaps clinically insane people do for fun? Probably not at this point, but I just tried to do what they could do. I was the little kid of the group.

One Sunday, they informed me that they were going to the track for a run. I had not set foot on a track since high school when we ran for the President's Physical Fitness test. The track is what—a quarter mile long, right? How hard could it be to run in circles around it? Well, let's just say that many experiences are vastly colored by those with whom you surround yourself. I should have known these guys wouldn't just jog around the track. They'd run up the stadium stairs, too. Then around the track some more. Then, guess what? More stadium stairs. This was when I invented the stadium escalator. My idea. Don't steal it.

Running is something that has never, *ever,* been even remotely easy for me. Put on one scuba flipper and run on a trampoline covered in ball bearings. That's what I think I looked like when I ran. Things jiggled and bounced like a couple of dogs fighting in a sleeping bag, and my legs always felt itchy. Still haven't figured that one out. Let's not even talk about the fact that my heart felt like it was going climb out of my rib cage and physically attack me. I was not going fast, but at least I was moving. The rest of the group looked like gazelles compared to my slow, lurching gait. They flowed up and down the stairs effortlessly. I was trying hard not to beat myself up for being so slow when I found myself running alongside Anna on the track. Mental fist pump. *Woohoo! I am NOT the slowest person here, after all! Someone else is running with me*! A few minutes later Anna said, "Oh, yeah, I'm pregnant, so I have to keep my heart rate really low." I glanced down at my watch and thought, "I wonder if anyone has ever intentionally thrown up on a pregnant woman." Since I couldn't actually talk at that point to formulate a coherent response, I just smiled and nodded.

When we finally stopped, someone with a super-advanced watch announced that we had run eight miles. Eight MILES? Are you kidding me? No wonder my legs felt like empty skin tubes. Eight miles was a really, *really long* way to run.

I spent the next couple of weeks doing some one-on-one lessons with my friend, Keith. I was painfully aware of how *uncool* I was on my road bike with the triple chain ring and reflectors, not to mention that I was wearing tennis shoes and using toe cages. The cool kids all rode sleek carbon-fiber frame bikes. They always seemed to match, even down to their socks. It wasn't about the fashion or even a desire to fit in. I just wanted to *get better,* and these people knew what they were doing. I'll take free education anywhere I can get it.

Keith and I would practice clipping in and out in the empty parking lots at Stone Mountain. This reminded me of my first driving lessons with my dad, who wouldn't let me operate a vehicle on the road until I proved myself by driving in an empty church parking lot—except when I stopped the car, I didn't spaz out and fall over.

The interesting thing about training with a group of triathletes who are training for an Ironman is that you have no baseline idea of what is normal and what is not. In my frame of reference, every triathlete was training for an Ironman, because triathletes do Ironman races. I was completely ignorant of the fact that many athletes spend years preparing and building their bodies to reach this volume. I figured if the group was going out to ride a certain distance, I might as well join them. Another saying comes to mind—*If you're gonna be dumb, you'd better be tough.*

After the exhausting 18-mile ride at Stone Mountain, the group invited me to join them for a 40-mile trek at the Silver Comet Trail. The Silver Comet Trail is a mixed-use running, riding, and hiking path that is closed to traffic. It is a former railroad track that runs from Smyrna, Georgia, to Alabama and back. Free from cars, it's one of the safest places to ride in Atlanta. Forty miles may as well have been forty decibels for all it meant to me. Sometimes you don't ask questions, because you literally know so little that you don't even know what questions to ask. They invited me, so they must think I can do it, right?

When the weekend rolled around, we were experiencing typical Georgia fall weather with temperatures in the 60s one weekend, 40s the next. This happened to be a weekend where it was in the 40s. This posed a bit of a problem, as I had never ridden outside in the cold. Bailing on the ride wasn't an option, so I just threw on a long-sleeve T-shirt and some yoga pants.

I arrived at the ride and got out of my car. Vanessa and Anna eyed me skeptically. Kelly asked me if that was what I was going to wear. That was a little like a doctor asking, *have you always had this thing growing out of your skull? Ummmm....sure?!* They looked at each other and started digging through their cars looking for proper attire. Someone produced a pair of gloves, while someone else gave me a hat. Because I had zero concept of how long a 40-mile ride would take (or the difference between 44° still air and 44° in a 15-mph wind, for that matter), I had packed one bottle of water, and that was it. Someone else dug out some form of nutrition that contained calories.

It didn't take long for me to realize that *BOOT CUT* anything and bikes do not mix. The bottom of my pants began to get tangled up between my crank and the chain of the bike. My pants were getting shredded, and I was obviously never going to last 40 miles that way. I stopped and tucked the bottom of my pants into my socks. There was no denying I was a newbie at this point. I felt about as ridiculous as I looked. In addition to my clothing being ripped up, I was freezing. My long sleeve T-shirt provided zero protection against the cold, damp morning. I wanted to stop, but no amount of discomfort seemed worse to me than the idea of giving up. (I was noticing as I continued doing things I didn't know I could do, that this trait was becoming more dominant in me.) So I tucked my pants into my socks and kept on pedaling.

At the 20-mile mark, I had a real *come to Jesus* moment with myself. This was the farthest I had ever ridden, and I was now 20 miles from my frickin' car with only my bike and my dead legs to get me back. I cursed at myself in my head for being stupid enough to think I could ride this distance. I couldn't believe we were turning around and going back. I was exhausted, hungry, and thirsty. I tried eating the bar someone gave me, only to fumble with the package and drop it. I was already so far behind the group that I didn't want to hold anyone up by stopping to retrieve it, so I let it go. I was getting angry—surely these seasoned athletes had to know that it was ridiculous to invite me to ride 40 miles!! Were they trying to kill me? I was completely shelled by the time I made it back to the car, and I thought about leaving my bike there for someone who likes this crap. Kelly dug out a blueberry scone that she had bought from Starbucks that morning. I *cannot stand scones,* but at that particular moment, it was the most delicious thing I could have possibly eaten. I was on the verge of tears, I was so upset—though not really at anyone in particular as much as at the situation. I wasn't expecting to be a superstar cyclist overnight, but I also didn't think it would be this painful and difficult. If the rest of the group kept riding week after week—even longer distances than this—there must be some trick to making it more tolerable. No one else seemed to be as cold and miserable as I was. Certainly not as humiliated.

It took me a full hour before any of the feeling returned to my feet. Once I thawed out, I went directly to my local bike store, purchasing cold-weather tights, gloves, base layers, shoe covers, and a hat. I threw a windbreaker and rain jacket in there for good measure. You cannot predict the weather, but you can be one thing…prepared. If I was going to completely screw up another bike ride, it was going to be based on my conditioning, not my ignorance. After all, it's riding bikes! It's supposed to be fun!

This new form of training was very different from what my body was accustomed to. Sure, I did cardio, but really I was just a meathead who loved to lift weights. This was hard, but a different type of hard. Maybe *challenging* is the right word. I would wake up the day after training with a heavy, lactic acid induced feeling in my legs. Instead of taking off days, we would swim for recovery. My body was starting to lean out, and my appetite was completely insane. I was still practicing the habits I had developed to shed the 70 pounds: portion control, smaller, more frequent meals, lots of fruits and veggies as snacks, reduced processed foods and refined sugars. I was demanding more of my body than I ever had, and it was asking for more from me in return. The higher training volume gave me some more flexibility in how I ate, and I was now able to be a little less strict while enjoying the same benefits.

Almost immediately after meeting this group of triathletes and reading my first issue of *Triathlete* magazine, I knew a triathlon would be in my future. I was going to become a *triathlete!* I just didn't know where to start. There are as many plans and opinions as there are magazines and people. The group I was training with was made up of seasoned triathletes, and I learned quickly that I needed to figure out my own level of training. Before I even realized it, their 40-mile rides had turned into 80-milers. They were kind, and they let me tag along, but the truth was that I was holding them back, and I knew it. Total immersion into the culture of triathlon was how I decided that I would learn best.

Soon I was applying anti-friction cream to places I never thought would chafe (which cut down dramatically on the amount of screaming during the post-workout shower) and eating weird little packets of gooey stuff like it was normal. Tan lines started to develop on my legs from riding outside. It became normal to see completely hairless men riding bicycles that cost more than my car. *Working out* was now replaced with the word *training*. "Bricks" were no longer small rectangular blocks made of clay, but a word used to describe a run done immediately following a bike ride. A fartlek had nothing to do with flatulence and everything to do with running intervals. I was talking the talk; now all I needed to do was walk the walk. It was time to pull the trigger and sign up for something!

I found a local duathlon about 45 minutes from my house and a super-sprint triathlon about two hours away in Alabama. My entry fees were paid, and I was in. I even joined the USA-Triathlon Association. A *du*athlon is different from a *tri*athlon in that the format is run-bike-run as opposed to swim-bike-run. For someone who didn't like running, this seemed like an unlikely first race, but doing things that don't come naturally to me was becoming a way of life. Plus, it was inexpensive and local, so I went with it.

The morning of my first race arrived much sooner than I was ready for. The granny gear that once adorned my bike had been removed along with my reflectors. I kept the basket on the handlebars because you never know when you'll find a puppy or a bunny (kidding, but I do love some puppies!). I now had a water bottle cage to hold fluids and a small bike computer that told me how fast and far I had ridden, even when I didn't feel like knowing.

I showed up for my first race excited to see what all the fuss was about. A couple of my training partners came and gave me reassurance that everything would go fine. I wasn't totally aware at that point that people wore things referred to as *tri kits*. A tri kit is a skintight outfit that has a limited amount of padding in the shorts. It's designed to be functional for the swim, then to wear on the bike and run. Triathlon clothing still felt weirdly foreign on my body, pinching me in all the wrong places. I opted to wear regular bike shorts and a riding top.

I put my bike in the rack in the transition area and prepped my running gear. I then warmed up and got myself ready to start. To say that I was anxious would be putting it mildly. This wasn't a large race, but it was the first time I was competing in anything athletic since the eleventh grade. It was also the first time I was *racing* as an individual. All my previous sports endeavors involved being on a team. People started to take their positions at the start line. I wasn't sure where to position myself. Clearly, I was not going to be at the forefront of the race, yet I eyed some older folks, who looked like they would just get in my way.

The race director played the national anthem, made some race announcements, and counted us down to a start... 5, 4, 3, 2, 1 ...WHHOOONK. Off went the horn along with the tiny chirps of everyone's watch. Knowing very little about pacing, I did what everyone else did—take off like we were being chased by a pack of wolves. It didn't take long for my heart rate to accelerate and the lactic acid to start accumulating in my legs. Slowing to a pace that I knew was possible to maintain, I backed off and slowly began getting passed. After a 5k run, it was time for the fun to start...the bike! Having very little to gauge my abilities against in training, I was happy to see that I passed people on the bike. By the time the second run rolled around, I came up with a theory why running after a ride is called a brick—because your legs are made of bricks, you have bricks in your pockets, several people are smashing you with bricks, and its raining bricks. There's not really any way to describe it. Just go ride a bike until your legs are really tired and then try to run. You will convince yourself it is impossible until you convince yourself otherwise. I forced myself to make my legs move, despite their unfathomable weight, and trudged my way through the final two-mile run.

Crossing the finish line felt absolutely amazing. It is the kind of satisfaction that can only come from hard work. I had finished a race completely by myself, and that sense of accomplishment is something that I will never forget.

After the race, two women came up to me and asked if I was racing in the Athena category. "Athena?" I responded, questioning them. They explained that people who are of a certain size get their own special category in triathlons and duathlons. It's like their way of saying, *we know how hard it must be to chase down those twigs, so you get to compete with people who are your own size. Ummm...thanks...? After losing seventy pounds, I actually thought I **was** a twig!*

Imagine my surprise when the announcer called my name as the winner of the female 20–24 category. I raced and I WON something?! How awesome was that? Who did I beat out? Can't wait to look and...oh. The 20–24 category consisted entirely of Danielle Grabol. So I didn't beat anyone. Also didn't get beaten...so there's that. It took away a bit from my level of excitement but only fueled the competitive fire that was starting to burn inside me. I compared my times to other race categories to see where I would have placed, and knew I was absolutely hooked.

A month later, I traveled to Birmingham, Alabama, to compete in my first triathlon. Geared toward beginners, this event held the swim portion in a pool. It was one of the shortest and least intimidating distances I could find, with a 200-yard swim, 10-mile bike, and 3-mile run.

For someone who was training for such a short race, I was putting a lot of time and energy into my preparation. Keith would drag me to Stone Mountain and make me do hill repeats on the bike and then run the hilly five-mile loop around the mountain. I marveled at the volume of work my friends would put in to train for their Ironman. Since the training was becoming fun and social for me, I didn't mind doing more than I needed to do. Running was still not something I particularly enjoyed (or was very good at), so naturally I had a tendency to do what I was the best at—biking. Swimming was hard for me, too. I was by no means a natural, but I didn't find it quite as intolerable as running.

As dumb luck would have it, a couple of weeks before my big debut I came down with some type of respiratory infection. Getting sick was not a part of my master plan of becoming a triathlete. I went to the doctor, and he diagnosed me with walking pneumonia. Since I had the *walking* version and not the bedridden version, I figured it was okay to travel and race. It's just pneumonia, right?

The morning of the race I was so excited to finally become a triathlete! I am not a terribly patient person, so training for anything for a time period that lasted more than a month seemed like forever. Thus, I was excited to *finally* become a triathlete.

The pool swim was manageable, but the bike course was much harder than I anticipated. My lungs felt heavy, and I couldn't get enough air, almost as if I had a respiratory infection that could kill me.

The run was a disaster. I was coughing and hacking all over the place. I crossed the finish line and promptly began coughing so violently that I barfed right in front of God and everybody. I scored zero style points, but none of that mattered because—I. WAS. A. TRIATHLETE!

I love it when people tell me that they want to train for their first triathlon. Nothing can ever take the place of the excitement and fulfillment of crossing that first finish line! It can be overwhelming when people start thinking about all the gear they need to race. I suggest that you be modest in your investments at first. If you think triathlon is prohibitive in cost, think about ways you can save money. Triathletes love to upgrade their bikes, so maybe you can purchase a used bike? Local triathlon stores will often offer an entry-level package that includes a bike, shoes, and helmet, etc. Ask if they want to sell demo wheels or bikes. End-of-year sales are also a great way to get a deal on a bike when the newer models are about to debut. Before you invest a lot of money on high-end gear, make sure that triathlon is something you want to do more than once or twice.

If you do choose to hire a coach or even have a mentor, make sure you are a good fit—not just familiar with your fitness or race goals, but your work life and your personality. Also, when you decide to use a coach or mentor, listen to them and DO WHAT THEY SAY. A couple of reasons for this— one is that you may be paying them, and if you aren't doing what they say you are wasting your money, and that is stupid. Another is that there are as many opinions on everything related to training as there are people with mouth holes out of which to spew them. Most of it is well-intentioned, decent advice, but there is no need to confuse yourself or risk screwing up a good thing by adding in unknown quantities. Simply say, "Hmm, I'll ask my coach," and ask your coach. If he or she is a good coach, they will take the time to explain to you why a suggestion will or won't work for you.

Training for a triathlon can be overwhelming, regardless of the distance. Look for a local triathlon club to join that hosts group workouts. Not only is riding in groups safer, but also they will be able to help you with what to expect, transition clinics, etc. The decision on whether to hire a coach is highly personal. Some people want and/or need the one-on-one attention, motivation, and support. Hiring a coach isn't just for the elite or extremely fast triathlete these days. It is also not required to perform well, or even to finish a triathlon.

The most important thing you can do is to remember that this is a hobby and that you are doing it for FUN!

3

BROKEN, NEVER BREAKING

People are always blaming their circumstances for what they are. I don't believe in circumstances. The people who get on in this world are the people who get up and look for the circumstances they want, and, if they can't find them, make them.

—George Bernard Shaw

Each November, Panama City Beach, Florida, is home to the largest Ironman triathlon in the Southeast. The beach that is normally known for wild parties and binge drinking becomes home to a different type of party that involves an entirely different kind of abuse to one's body— 140.6 miles of human-powered movement.

It was November 2006, and I was nearing the end of my first season of participating in triathlon. I had raced a handful of sprints and one Olympic distance race. I had signed up to run the Publix Marathon during the upcoming month of March and was excited to have something to focus on that winter once the official race season was over. Keith and many other friends were racing their first full Ironman, and I was beyond excited to go to Panama City Beach and watch my first long-distance race and cheer them on. We arrived the Wednesday prior to Saturday's race day. The town was awash with veiny, sinewy, shaved, single-digit body fat-type people, riding what they claimed were bicycles but looked like alien spacecraft. Large signs were posted for everyone to see—*Warning: Large Triathlon on November 4th. Beware of Cyclists and Runners on Roads*.

Keith, Olga, Eduardo, and I checked into our condo and decided that we would ride our bikes the two miles to the Athlete Check-in and Expo area. Though I don't remember much about the Expo at all, I'll never forget the ride back to the condo. The light turned green, and we all took off after a brief stop. Generally, I was afraid to ride in the back of any pack, so Keith would *always* ride behind me. But today my shoe wouldn't clip into the pedal, so the trio took off ahead of me while I kicked and mumbled curse words and slowly got moving.

Less than five minutes later, I heard a sound that I can only describe as a cacophony of violence…glass breaking, things cracking, metal and plastic scraping across other metal and plastic—just general chaos. I then felt the impact of my body as I landed in a gravel parking lot and rolled to a stop. Bewildered, I sat up and looked down at my feet, and what I saw didn't make any sense at all. My left leg was completely deformed with my foot twisted in a way that would make Gumby cringe. Strangers had all stopped in their tracks and people were screaming for help and running toward me. I heard people yelling and saw my friends pointing and screaming, "Stop that guy!"

I had just been hit by a car.

Everyone told me not to move, which wasn't necessary, as I was not in the best shape to scamper off. I spent a couple of moments trying to wrap my mind around the most traumatic thing that had happened to me in my entire life. A large crowd quickly formed around me. People were making a lot of commotion and stating that they saw the guy hit me. It was totally his fault. He claimed he didn't see me, so no one can say it was malicious or intentional, but the part where you hit a human being on a bike hard enough to shatter your windshield and never hit your brakes and then run over her bike and only stop because the splintered remains of the bike frame flattened two tires *and then* decide to try to outrun a bunch of pissed off triathletes on foot…well, that takes you into a new realm of stupidity-induced problems.

I recall him standing over me, staring at me in sheer panic. He was smoking a cigarette and trying to touch me. Apologizing profusely he appeared to be under the influence of something. I asked that someone please get him away from me, as the smell was disgusting.

I knew my leg was broken the second I saw it. Your leg just doesn't look like that without it being shattered inside. Oddly, I felt no pain, but figured it was going to get very real when the adrenaline wore off. I asked about my bike, although I knew it was a goner. I couldn't assess the condition of rest of my body; I could tell by the look on the bystanders' faces, and the quiet whispers of *Oh, my God,* that the rest of me wasn't in great shape, either. Olga was softly crying as she tried to comfort me.

I was loaded into the ambulance, and the EMT asked me what hurt. Suddenly, I started to feel this terrible pain underneath my pinkie finger. I looked down to see a small rock embedded underneath my skin and my fingernail. I replied, "My pinky hurts." It is strange how the body seems to prioritize things sometimes. It was like my own body was trying to dangle keys in front of my face to distract me—*Hey, pay no attention to your blood-dripping leg; *jingle jingle* look at this tiny pebble under your fingernail!* The EMT asked, "Is that it?" Instead of answering, I started telling her that I was glad to be alive and recounted the story about my friend Victor's brother, who was hit by a car and passed away. She kept asking about my pain, and I would reply, "I'm alive." The EMT finally said, "You're in shock, Sweetie."

The paramedics were correct; I was in shock. It soon wore off, and the most unbelievable pain I had ever felt was coursing through my body. The tiniest movement hurt, and when they lifted the stretcher out and placed it on the ground, it was almost more than I could take. I arrived at the hospital where they cut my clothing off of me. When I hit the ground, I had the misfortune of landing in a gravel parking lot. I looked like I had gone down a cheese-grater slip-n-slide, and hundreds of tiny pebbles had been forced under my skin. It's hard to remember where the pain started first, but as soon as the shock wore off, it was all encompassing. I was flooded with feelings of pain, anger, fear, and gratitude for being alive and conscious.

X-rays determined that my left fibula and tibia were shattered. The orthopedic surgeon on call came in and told me that he would need to operate to repair my leg. My only question was, "Do you think I can still run my marathon in March?" The surgeon (who I assume was trained not to laugh at ridiculous questions) replied, "Your leg is completely shattered. I don't know if you will ever run again. We will do our best to repair it, but we cannot guarantee that you won't need an additional surgery to remove the rod and screws and that you won't have any leg length discrepancies." Though the physical pain was starting to increase, his words were just as painful. *How much time and work had I devoted to this goal? How much had I already worried about this exact thing happening to me? After all of this, am I going to have to start over?*

My road rash was so intense that they put me to sleep so I wouldn't have to endure the agony of being awake while someone picked road debris out of my skin. They scheduled my surgery for the following morning, and calls were made to my family and a few friends back in Atlanta. Nothing was really sinking in at that point. My mother was already on her way to Panama City from Atlanta.

Following my surgery, I spent several days in the hospital recuperating from the rest of my injuries. My left hip appeared to have taken the initial impact with the car, as it got so swollen that my mom had to buy larger clothes for me to wear. They feared I had developed a blood clot. Fortunately, I had not, and they started me on heparin, a blood thinner, to reduce my risk of developing a clot from being sedentary.

I am not a very agreeable patient, because I don't like being unable to manage things on my own. I was completely helpless and had to use a walker to get around. It was excruciatingly painful to move even an inch. I was hooked up to a morphine pump to help manage the pain. I pressed it once and it made me vomit, so I didn't press it again. The nurse came in the next day and looked at the report.

"You know that you can use this every six minutes, right?"

"Yes," I replied.

"So why did you only use it once?" she inquired.

"It made me throw up," I explained.

"So why didn't you call us and ask for something else?"

"I don't like throwing up."

It didn't take very long before the pain became unbearable, and I gladly took the nurses up on other options for pain medications.

Friday came, and I asked if I would be able to watch the Ironman the following day. My mom was obviously and appropriately appalled at the idea, and the hospital explained that they weren't ready to release me; if I wanted to watch the race, I would have to leave AMA (against medical advice). I desperately wanted to watch my friends' race. A little later, Keith told me that he wasn't going to compete. This was really upsetting, and I begged him to do his race. He was rattled by the accident and didn't think he'd be able to keep his head where it needed to be. To this day, I think he feels some guilt that I was riding in the back of the group. The reality is, however, that the doctor said the reason I survived the impact had a lot to do with my size. Both Keith and Olga are much smaller than I am, and my doctors said that both of them would have come away from that accident with more injuries than I had. It's easy to run various scenarios through your mind after something like this happens, but there is a reason I was riding in the back of the group and a reason it was me that was hit by the car.

After spending five long days in the hospital, I was ready to travel back to Atlanta. I had recently rescued a small hound-mix puppy named Poncey, he had traveled with us and was being boarded. I missed him so much and was happy to be reunited with him—until the moment that he jumped on me, and I thought, "I wonder if anyone has ever intentionally vomited on a rescue puppy."

The ride home was horrible. I tried to lie down in the back seat of my mom's car but was unable to get comfortable. I swear Mom hit every pothole between Panama City Beach and Atlanta. I cried out in pain repeatedly, begging her to drive slower and stop hitting things.

I was living in a two-story townhouse at the time, without a full bathroom downstairs. Stairs were out of the question, so Martha, the owner of my company, graciously offered me her carriage house to stay in. When I arrived in Atlanta, my best friend Karen was waiting for me. "You smell horrible," she complained. "Glad to see you, too. Let's just say I've had better days."

Karen insisted that I shower and helped my mom and another friend lower me into the bathtub. It was the first time since the accident I had more than a sponge bath. They gently washed my body, making sure no soap got into the many spots where I was missing skin. Getting out of the tub took some clever maneuvering with one leg. Just the simple act of cleaning myself took the help of two people and left me more exhausted than any workout I could remember.

My mom spent the first few nights there caring for me and for Poncey. It was not easy for either of us—on one hand, I was filled with gratitude that I was alive and would be okay. On the other hand, I was very angry. *Why had this happened to me? What did I do to deserve this?*

I would become easily frustrated and snap at my mom, who was merely trying to help.

Several friends stopped by to see me throughout the days that followed. They would wheel me down the street in a portable wheelchair if it was nice outside, but most days I just laid in bed. Poncey lay close to my broken leg between his occasional fits of puppy terror. He would growl at anyone who came too close to me.

Everything I tried to do was completely exhausting to my body. Getting up and getting myself to the bathroom while using a walker was incredibly tiring. My appetite was gone, and my muscles were getting soft. Olga called me one day to check in on me and told me about a 60-mile bike ride that she had just finished. As soon as I hung up the phone, I burst into tears. I wanted nothing more than what had just a year or so earlier been so torturous to endure. I'd have given almost anything to ride a bike. I desperately wanted to be better.

After a few weeks of recuperating at Martha's, I went back home. This proved to be a lot more difficult than I thought it would be. We take for granted that our homes are suited for us, and that under normal conditions we can navigate them easily. Able-bodied people rarely envision a scenario in which they will *need* assistive devices. My bathroom was too narrow for my walker. I had to take one hop inside the room, then turn sideways and shimmy myself to the toilet. To get up the stairs, I had to hop on one leg, holding onto the banister with one hand and the wall with the other. Since I couldn't carry anything in my hands and hold onto the wall and banister at the same time, I would wear a small sling-pack to transport things like a bottle of water and my phone up and down the stairs. With every hop it would whack the back of my head. If I got all the way upstairs and realized I had forgotten something, it was just too bad.

Gone were the days of just *running* downstairs. I planned all my movements up and down the stairs carefully and was still paranoid that my spastic puppy was going to take me out. He often mistook my one-legged hop as me trying to play, so he would jump on me in return. If you ever want to know how infuriatingly inconvenient it is to live like this, take a mattress off of a twin bed, soak it in a swimming pool until it is just as heavy and unwieldy as it can be, and carry it around with you everywhere you go for a day.

I started going stir crazy once some of my energy returned. I wasn't allowed to drive and was totally dependent on everyone for everything, right down to doing my laundry. Being helpless is not something I excel at (and maybe the one thing I am okay not excelling at). I took up cross- stitching and learned I didn't have the patience. I would insist on going to the grocery store with my mom, even if it meant I was in the electric scooter. Against her wishes, I also insisted that she drive me to the gym. "What are you going to do?" she asked. "I can swim!" I replied. They had opted to give me a boot instead of a hard cast, which meant I could take it on and off as needed for showering, etc. I made sure to ask permission to swim and was given the green light by my doctor, as long as I used a pull buoy.

The first thing I realized when I got to the gym was that the doors there didn't open automatically. I stood with my walker for several minutes until someone opened the door for me. The woman's locker room never seemed that far away until I tried to navigate there hopping on one leg while keeping my other leg dangling with a boot on it. Hop…hop…hop…thankfully, I wasn't in a hurry to get there. The boot was starting to get heavy. I've seen fancy walkers that have a place for your leg to rest, but in 2006, my walker just had me dangling my awkward boot as I hobbled from place to place.

After what seemed like an eternity, I finally made it to the locker room—pouring sweat and exhausted. Hopping on one leg for that long took everything out of me, but getting in the pool itself was also a task. I swam a couple hundred yards and was completely wrecked. If I went another fifty, they would have to lift me out with a helicopter and drop me in my driveway, and that seemed logistically complicated and expensive, so I used the last tiny bit of my energy to get out.

Four weeks earlier, I was in the best shape of my life, signed up for a marathon, and felt amazing. Then with the flick of a cigarette lighter, my life was permanently changed. Although I will never know for sure, I assume that the person who hit me was under the influence of drugs and/or alcohol and was distracted while lighting a cigarette. He was charged with reckless driving and DUI. When I think about the fact that a driver hit me going over 40 mph and didn't touch the brakes, I realize how lucky I am to just be alive. There is no doubt in my mind that my bicycle helmet saved my life. Investing in a nicer, carbon helmet seemed ridiculous at the time, but this layer of carbon is what saved me. My helmet was cracked—my head was not.

After a few weeks of using the walker, I was strong enough to graduate to crutches. I was also given permission to start driving again. My newfound freedom left me wanting to get out and do things. I was attending school at Georgia State University, a large school located in downtown Atlanta. My first day back at school, I was quickly reminded how ill-equipped the school was for students who were not fully able to open doors for themselves or maneuver staircases. Getting from one building to another on crutches was nearly impossible, given the tight time frame I had between classes. When I registered, I was *able-bodied* and assumed I would be able to walk and easily make it to classes on time. Instead, I was regularly arriving 15 to 20 minutes late for classes, soaked in sweat, frustrated, and embarrassed. Unable to modify my schedule, I ended up dropping classes and taking online courses in their place. I loved school and missed the interaction of the classroom setting, but this was one of those times when I had to adapt to what was in front of me.

While most days I felt defined by what I was *unable* to do, I also had moments when I forgot that I was using crutches. One such time found me at a Starbucks. I ordered a drink, just like anyone else would do. I stood at the pickup counter and realized that I had no way to carry a drink out with me. Normally, I would put things in my knapsack, but the first thing you learn about putting a hot latte in your knapsack is never to put a hot latte in your knapsack. Being the proud person that I was, I didn't want to ask for help. When the barista called my name, he immediately realized I wasn't able to carry the drink and graciously offered to help me.

I hated needing help.

Routine X-rays were part of my post-surgical follow up to see how my leg was progressing. My doctor was pleased to see that it was heal-ing well and faster than the surgeon in Florida predicted. In March of 2007, I was allowed to start bearing some weight on my leg. My doctor gave me *percentages,* which of course were impossible to calculate. Instead, I used my pain as an indicator that I was bearing too much weight. Being able to put my left leg on the ground made using crutches much easier and allowed me to get around faster. Four months of holding my leg up had caused me to start having pain in my hip and back area.

Although I had not been a triathlete for very long, all I wanted was to race again. I longed for my body to heal, because I missed my friends and the community that I had grown to love so quickly. Becoming so obsessed with triathlon so quickly after my weight loss meant that I defined every part of myself as a *triathlete.* Having that ripped away from me left me empty. It was also an important lesson in balance; I knew that I was defined by much more than merely being a *triathlete,* but as humans we all want what we cannot have, and all I wanted was to be a triathlete again.

I wasn't surprised that I missed riding my bike, but I knew things were desperate when I started wishing I could run again. The one thing I had spent the most time complaining about the previous year suddenly became important to me. I *had* to run again, and I promised never to whine about it.

When the doctor told me that my racing days were behind me, I knew he was wrong. There would be a way, and I would find it. If there wasn't a way, I would create a way. It never crossed my mind that I wouldn't race or run again. Instead my thoughts were only on *how* I was going to make it happen. My brain has a wonderful way of minimizing injuries and obstacles while my body didn't quite understand why I wouldn't just rest and recover!

The longer I was unable to ride and run, the more important my recovery became to me. My legs had atrophied, and I started to worry about all the fitness I had lost. My friends, Bob and Sue, had a Compu-Trainer® set up in their garage and invited me over to ride, right leg only, while they trained. I appreciated so much that my triathletc friends had not forgotten about me. They checked in on me, brought me meals, walked my puppy, and reassured me that I would make a full recovery, which filled me with optimism.

When I was finally released to bear full weight on my leg and not use crutches or the boot, I was like a kid on Christmas morning. I called my mom, thrilled to share my news.

"Mom! I can WALK! Do you want to go to Stone Mountain?" I asked. "Sure," she replied, "but you aren't going to try to walk around the mountain are you?" Mom clearly knew me.

"Absolutely! Why not?" I replied, knowing full well that there were a million reasons why a hilly five-mile walk was a terrible idea, but not being interested in hearing a single one of them.

It took me three hours to walk five miles. My mom left me, and I limped to my car in excruciating pain. As if out of the soundtrack of a movie, as I was finishing my sufferfest, the song, *Everybody Hurts,* by REM, came on my iPod. I couldn't think of a more appropriate theme song for my first workout back.

Patience isn't a virtue I have much of, and I pushed my recovery much faster than I should have. My leg would respond by swelling and causing me terrible pain. My hip was never quite right, and an MRI determined that I had suffered a herniated disc in my lower back. Six months of relying only on my right leg had resulted in significant imbalances in strength.

In May of 2007, seven months after breaking my leg, I went to a local track to do my first run. I intentionally went to a track that I knew would be empty. No one wanted to see the failfest I was about to put on display, and I sure as hell didn't want anyone to see it. Running was not something I was ever good at, so my expectations for today's run were low. I started my Garmin watch and made four incredibly tough laps around the track in 12 minutes and 30 seconds. I couldn't have run any faster if I tried. I sat down on the track and cried. I was so thankful to be running again; overcome with joy to run the slowest mile I had ever run while knowing that it was a miracle to be running at all.

The remainder of the summer of 2007 was spent trying to get the courage to ride comfortably outside and race on open roads. The first group ride I went on after the accident caused me to have a panic attack. I pulled over on the side of the road and wept to Keith, convinced that a car had almost hit me.

In August of 2007, I decided that I was going to sign up for Ironman Louisville, to be held in August of 2008. I had never raced anything longer than an Olympic distance triathlon. Running was not easy, and I still walked with a limp. I didn't have a plan, but I knew I wanted to do an Ironman. Keith signed up too, as well as a handful of our other training partners.

I'm not sure signing up for a 140.6-mile race was really something my doctor would have recommended at that point (not that I would have listened anyway). Once the euphoria of registering for my first Ironman wore off, I realized that I had work to do! I picked Ironman Louisville because it was driving distance from Atlanta but neglected to pay attention to the fact that it was a hilly course and would be hot and humid in Kentucky in August. I choose it simply because my only other option for an Ironman within driving distance was Florida, and I wasn't particularly crazy about the idea of having an experience as special as my first Ironman shared with the city were my accident had occurred.

In May of 2008, I traveled back to Panama City Beach for the first time since my accident. I raced my first half Ironman, the Gulf Coast Half. The bike course required that I ride down the exact same road where my accident had happened. Seeing the gravel parking lot I landed in made me realize just how fortunate I was. Being able to return here and race 70.3 miles was a miracle, and I was thankful for the opportunity and my recovery. I was overcome with anxiety being on the same road I had suffered such pain on, yet so grateful to be alive. Tears streamed down my face as I realized it was a miracle that I was alive. My skin will never look the same as it did prior to my accident. I have scars on both my legs, and the left one has a huge bump in it where the bone overgrew when it was healing. Yet despite these physical imperfections, I know it could have been much, much worse. While my bones healed, I could not look at my legs without the constant reminder of the accident, and the grateful feeling.

My accident also gave me a small glimpse into what it's like for people who live with disabilities and the struggles they face daily. Just the simple act of using a walker to get around created challenges almost every place I went. Without automatic buttons that pushed doors open, I would have to stand and stare at doors, waiting for someone to realize I needed assistance. My own home lacked the modifications that I needed to be able to live there and care for myself. While I was fortunate that my injuries healed and I could function independently, it still forced me to think about those who could not.

In August of 2008, 21 months after my accident, I toed the line at Ironman Louisville. To say I was nervous would be an extreme under-statement. My stomach did flip-flops all night. A 2.4- mile swim, 112-mile bike, and 26.2-mile run were ahead of me. My mom cried the entire day. I plunged into the Ohio River that morning, and 14 hours, 13 minutes, and 56 seconds later, I crossed the finish line (with Keith about 10 seconds behind me) and became an Ironman. The race was ugly—much harder than I anticipated or was physically prepared for. I had trained to the best of my ability, but I had underestimated the level of fitness required for 14 hours of racing. Sheer grit and determination were half the reason I finished that day. I will never forget the feeling of running down the finishing chute and having them announce, *Dani Grabol, YOU, are an Ironman!*

It took me several years to fully recover from my accident. Pain was a daily part of my life. I became so accustomed to my leg hurting in some capacity that the day I walked out my front door to walk my dogs and *nothing* hurt, it made me think something was wrong. For several years, I walked with the slightest limp. Intensive physical therapy, mas-sage work, chiropractic care, and strength work are what I credit with making a semi-full recovery, along with the refusal to accept anything less than a full recovery as an option.

In December of 2006, I would have told you that the accident was the worst thing that had ever happened to me. Now I think otherwise. I work with older adults, and my job requires that I have significant patience. Breaking my leg taught me the virtue of patience and empathy. It helped me to realize that everyone you meet is going through, or has emerged from, some type of struggle in their life. When you see someone at the gym who leaves a spin class halfway through, you might think, *that person gave up*, but they may be celebrating the fact that they made it halfway through something. Health is such a precious thing, and we often take it for granted until it is taken away from us. During my recovery, I would make deals. *If I can just race again, I promise to never complain about the training.* Of course, I still complained about the training, but nowhere near as much as other people seem to! I feel grateful for every day that I wake up and my feet hit the floor. Returning to any sort of athletic activity was humbling, yet my injury was one of the greatest gifts I could have received in my short athletic career. It taught me to be aware of what my body was going through. It put pain in context. What I once considered painful is now merely discomfort. Being injured gave me another level of motivation: a fire set deep inside that I never knew existed. Not only did I want my injuries to heal, but also I wanted to get better and be a triathlete again. I needed to race stronger and farther than I ever had before.

In 2008, an Ironman was the end-all of racing in triathlon for me. I was unaware that anything more existed. Soon that would change.

No one enjoys being injured. It is particularly difficult for athletes, as we find that so much of our identity is associated with our sport of choice. Injuries might be a result of overuse and your body's way of signaling you that you need to take a break and focus on something else, or they might be the result of something far beyond your control. Regardless of what caused the injury you have two choices, you can wallow in your misery or you can accept your situation for what it is and make a plan for how to overcome it. Could an injury end your athletic career? Absolutely, all the more reason why we should cherish our good health when we have it, and take full advantage of the wonderful abilities that we have to participate in things that we love.

4

Discovering Love and Ultras

We are all a little weird, and life is a little weird, and when we find someone whose weirdness is compatible with ours, we join up with them and fall in mutual weirdness and call it love.

—Dr. Seuss

As it turns out, if you have a severe break in your leg, you need more than 21 months to recover to the point of doing a full Ironman. I'd call that a pro tip, but in retrospect, it seems really obvious. Most of the year 2009 was spent paying for that mistake. Multiple issues starting cropping up, mostly my fault, as a result of layering too much training on a body with too many discrepancies in strength. IT band syndrome, piriformis syndrome, and the discovery that I had two herniated discs in my lower back as a result of the accident were just some of the issues that kept me in near constant pain and discomfort. My right leg was substantially stronger than my left—so much so that you could see the size difference in my calves! I continued to favor that leg when running and riding, and my left leg wasn't thrilled about me playing favorites.

Having signed up for a half Ironman, and realizing there was no way I would be able to race it while injured, forced me to really bring myself back to the basics of working out and strength development. I scrapped all plans of racing long course and focused on rehabbing my body more. Stretching became routine, along with more massage work and yoga practice. My weekly volume of training hours declined, and quality workouts became much more important than quantity.

I had been selected to race on a local triathlon store's race team. I met a group of triathletes who were much more seasoned than I was, extremely fast, and absolutely hilarious. The team atmosphere and back and forth banter were exactly what I needed. We traveled to local sprint distance triathlons, raced hard, and had fun. Sometimes we wore costumes and our races had themes. Getting on the podium was important, but so was having a really good time. We routinely wagered against each other, talked all sorts of trash on social media, and just had a generally great time racing. The social aspect of this sport cannot be overstated if you are the kind of person who enjoys the group dynamic.

I had struck up a friendship with a guy on the team named Jason. Tall, bald, tattooed, opinionated, and obnoxious was my first impression. It took me a long time to warm up to him and figure out he wasn't really that terrible after all. After we became friends on Facebook, I did the obligatory profile picture swipe through—it's not stalking—where I found a picture of him racing with his arm in a sling. Seriously?! This guy did a triathlon with his arm in a sling!? What a moron! That's like training for a full Ironman less than two years after a devastating accident…oh…yeah. I couldn't tell if he was a dumbass or a badass. Either way, I was starting to like what he was made of.

The world wanted Jason and me to date far before we were ready for it. I remember going on a bike ride with a mutual friend one day. She saw Jason's truck, parked alone in a spot where no one else ever parked. She shook her head and said, "He always goes against the grain." Jason was becoming more and more appealing! Neither of us is particularly sensitive, and we tend to joke around and pick on each other quite a bit. Not everyone understands this sense of humor, and our joking could definitely be misconstrued as bickering. After hearing that we were going on our first date, one of Jason's riding buddies said, "Good luck." Despite (or possibly due in part to) our nonstop banter, our first date was a huge success. I felt really certain that with Jason, there wouldn't be much guessing—what I see is what I get.

I ultimately got way more than I bargained for.

Jason is the hardest working person I have ever known. He wants to excel at everything he does. He has won sprint triathlons and qualified for the Boston Marathon, then decided to switch gears to race long course and won a 500-mile bike race. If you hired him to sweep the streets, they would be the best-swept streets in the city. He tracked all of his workouts meticulously in a notebook. He will beat you at rock paper scissors. It didn't matter what it was; if it was difficult and challenging, Jason wanted to try it. Some people would find a personality like his to be highly intimidating. Me? I was totally jealous and in complete awe. I wanted to see if I could pick up a little more of that through osmosis or something. I encourage people to surround themselves with people who are strong where they are weak; he had this in spades but was also strong in places I just wanted to be stronger.

Many triathletes spend the majority of their time swimming, biking, or running. But Jason? He didn't discriminate. As long as it was painful, he wanted in on it. The more obscure the workout, the better. He did cross fit workouts in his back yard. We would take a row machine to the track and row, run, and climb stadium stairs. Once, I even found a kettlebell by the pool! I had already developed a love of all things seemingly impossible and challenging. Dating Jason only fueled the fire.

His work ethic and discipline were contagious. Suddenly I wanted to be the best at everything, too. Jason was always humble about what he had accomplished. He just always wanted a little bit more of what life had to offer. He never stayed comfortable, and once he conquered something, he would move on to another sport or distance. Being comfortable for most people is easy. It's what feels safe, but over the course of time it is actually dangerous. Doing what felt good was what ultimately caused me to come face to face with my mortality in Dr. Davidson's office not long ago. Jason was all about being outside that safe zone. I loved being with someone who was willing to put himself out there and explore the unknown.

Jason finished his first 50-mile run not too long after we met. A few weeks after we started dating, he asked me to come crew for him during a 12-hour mountain bike race he was doing in north Georgia. His friend, Crispin, was racing as well and needed someone to crew for him. I had no idea what to expect, but I was all in.

I loved crewing. I'm not a flowers and chocolate kind of girl…more of a sunscreen and CO_2 cartridges type. Standing in the woods for 12 hours waiting for the guy you're dating to swing by and grab a water bottle from me was my version of fun. It didn't take long for me to figure out that some of the guys in the shared tent space had no one helping them, so I took them under my crew wing and helped them out, too.

In addition to the benefit of Jason fixing everything I broke (this is a huge benefit in our relationship, as I tend to break all sorts of things), I found myself getting stronger and stronger training with him. An extremely talented swimmer, he pushed me in the pool with one-on-one lessons. He wrote workouts for me and pointed out my errors, working on perfecting my form. Being the slow one on rides made me insane, so I would turn myself inside out to try and keep up. We only saw each other once during the week, on Wednesdays, and our date night would always start off with a swim and gym workout before dinner. Weekends would consist of Jason picking me up for a bike ride, riding all day, getting cleaned up, then going out to dinner. I probably spent more time on a bike staring at Jason's behind in spandex then I did looking at his face for the first year of our relationship.

Somewhere in there, Jason passed the test. My dad, Keith, and my dogs all loved him. He was a keeper.

In the fall of 2010, we traveled to Cedar Point, Ohio, to race my second and Jason's fifth 140.6-mile race at Rev3 Cedar Point. Though the race was Ironman distance, it is not considered an official Ironman event, as it was owned and operated by Rev3. Dating Jason paid huge dividends in racing; I shaved nearly three hours off my previous 140.6 time at Ironman Louisville. Jason also had a huge PR (personal record) proving that love does make you faster! Cedar Point was a great course that finished in the famous Cedar Point theme park. We both enjoyed traveling to races together and exploring new towns.

I was getting an itch to try out an ultra run, which is defined as anything longer than a standard 26.2-mile marathon. We found a 50k run in New River, Virginia, that seemed like something I could manage. It was about six weeks after the Cedar Point race. I figured I would have all this base fitness and, since I had just run a marathon, what's adding a few more miles?

When I signed up for the 50k, I forgot that I didn't really run. The devil is in the details, as they say. To me a run was the thing that I had to do to get from the second transition to the finish line. Granted, I knew I should run to train for events, but every time I thought, "I should really run today," I would look at my bike, all lonely and pitiful, and go for a ride instead. Running was never particularly easy for me, so I always had a great excuse for not doing it. First of all, it hurt, and secondly, I wasn't good at it. Okay, just the two excuses…but both very good ones.

If there is anything that you learn from reading this I hope it's this: Train for the races you sign up for. I repeat…train for your races!

My foray into ultra-racing was u-g-l-y ugly. For the first ten miles, my brain said, "This is so gorgeous! It's all sunshine and rainbows! So pretty! I love running!" The next ten, it was saying, "Oh, man. My feet are starting to hurt. When did my legs take on the density of a dying star? Where is everyone else?" During the final 11 miles, I heard, "This was the worst mistake I have ever made. I'm pretty sure I am running on exposed bone." Needless to say, crossing the finish line was not triumphant or exciting to me. It was the hardest thing I had ever done, and I learned an important lesson about ultras—don't underestimate them!

Jason knew he wanted to run 100 miles and, like any good girlfriend, I encouraged and supported his decision to frolic in the woods for 24 hours. We didn't know much about how to train for 100-mile runs and didn't really know anyone who raced them. Jason decided he would run the Keys 100 in May 2011, a 100-mile run from Key Largo to Key West. He wanted to cut his teeth on something more local first, so he found a race called the GUTS Reactor Run, about 90 minutes from Atlanta. It was on technical and hilly terrain. He also applied to Umstead, a 100-mile run in Raleigh, North Carolina, to be held in April 2011 and was wait listed.

I asked Jason what he would do if he got into Umstead.

"I'll do all three," he replied.

"You're going to do three 100- milers in three months?" I cocked my head and looked at him.

Jason shrugged. "Sure, why not?" While any reasonable person could fill the Library of Congress with reasons not to do that, I knew better than to question his judgment.

The GUTS Reactor Run was in March of 2011, in the North Georgia Mountains. I was extremely nervous about crewing him for something so big. He had trained so hard, and I wanted him to do well, but I also wasn't sure I could stay awake all night. I had no idea what he would want to eat, and I wondered if we would be cold, hot, etc. Basically, I packed everything you could think of and more. I made checklists, signs for the racers, and spreadsheets to help myself keep track of what food I had given him and when. I had offered to assist my friends, Bob and Sue, who were racing the 50-miler as well. I printed up signs for our table with everyone's name so they could easily find their food. Then I laminated the signs…partly because I didn't want them to get wet, mostly because I loved using the laminator at work. It sounds cool and smells good.

I was so nervous the night before the race that I barely slept. Weather reports were not looking favorable, and we knew there was a strong possibility that it would be rainy and wet. I woke up around 2 a.m. to the sound of rainfall. A little rain was going to make this that much more fun!

Jason's brother, Steve, came up early in the race, and we sat in the freezing-cold rain, waiting for Jason to come in from either a 13 or 7 mile loop. Because the race was so local, many of our friends wanted to be witness to the pain and agony running 100 miles was sure to bring.

They signed up for shifts of pacing or running with the athlete to keep him from falling asleep, running off course, attacking trees and rocks during hallucinations, and other things that can happen when you push yourself beyond a certain point. We all had turns running different shifts from miles 50 to 100.

The conditions were brutal. It rained all day, and the course kept getting muddier and muddier. There is mud and then there is Georgia Red Clay, which can be like running on wet glass. People would come in from a loop of either 13 or 7 miles and be covered in mud. I was freezing in the tent and couldn't imagine how miserable they had to be; yet they had smiles on their faces, so I figured they were having fun! As the rain continued and the sun set, I figured most of our friends would bail on the pacing duties. Instead of bailing, they showed up earlier than planned to cheer for other racers out on the course. You're doing something right in life when seven of your friends show up and want to run in the wet, cold, and muddy conditions with you just to see you finish a 100-miler.

Racers dropped out of the race almost every lap. I had never seen anything like it. They took the bibs from everyone and hung them up outside the race director's tent. Everyone who ran a lap with Jason ended up falling at some point. Jason remained upright the entire time, finishing with a time of 21:41:47, which was good enough for second overall of the 17 people who finished. At 5 a.m., he was smiling and totally spotless, surrounded by his red-clay-caked friends.

We were hooked.

Most of my girlfriends thought I was crazy for staying awake for 24 hours in the cold rain while calling it good, quality time spent with my boyfriend. Fortunately for Jason, I am not a normal woman. I was so excited to be able to play a part in allowing him to make this dream come true. Without the support of a crew, ultra-racing is incredibly difficult. Many races won't allow you to participate without crew. Being able to help someone finish something they want that bad is really special. Helping the person you love complete something that's important to them is truly gratifying for both of us. While I love racing, crewing has proven to be one of the most gratifying and meaningful things I can do for others.

Jason got into the Umstead 100 in April. We traveled to Raleigh and met up with a friend, Chuck, who was racing his first 100, and his crew, Yvonne, Steve, and Brett. The race was 20 minutes from my dad's house, so we stayed with him.

As a Vietnam vet and former Marine, Dad isn't impressed easily, but he decided to come out and watch part of the race, so I took that to mean he was impressed.

My phone rang early on in the race.

Dad: "Hey I thought you told me this was a run?"

Me: "It is."

Dad: "All I see is people walking!"

Me: "Well, are you driving up a hill? Most people walk hills."

Dad: "Okay, yeah, that's it."

Five minutes later, my phone rings again.

Dad: "Hey, they let women into this thing?"

Me: "You're kidding right? Of course women are allowed!"

Dad showed up a few minutes later and started inspecting my carefully laid-out nutrition. He questioned everything and decided it was all a waste of money; I could just give him honey and bread instead.

After a few minutes, Jason came running through. We replenished his fluids and gave him some nutrition. I wrote down his lap time and what calories I gave him on spreadsheet on a clipboard.

Dad: "Now what?"

Me: "Now we wait for him to run another 12.5-mile loop. We should see him again in a little over two hours."

Dad: "Shit! Two hours?! I am not sitting around waiting on him. I'm leaving. See you at the house. Love you!"

Not everyone gets as excited about racing as we do. Anyone can do it, but it certainly isn't for everyone.

Jason had an amazing race, finishing in 18 hours and 29 minutes. He placed 14th overall out of 143 racers.

The following day, we woke up to find my dad looking at the race results.

Dad: "Hey, Jason, did you know the winner did a 14:07?"

Jason: "Yeah, he was super fast. And tiny."

Dad: "Fourteen hours? You came in three whole hours after he did!"

Jason: "Yep. He beat me by a lot."

Dad: "Son, that's not a beating, that's an ass-whooping!"

If Dad was impressed that Jason ran 100 miles at an 11-minute per mile pace, he had a really funny way of showing it.

Barely a month later, Jason, his brother Steve, good friend Jimmy, and I traveled to Key Largo. Georgia is hot in May, and then there is Florida hot. And then there is Florida Keys hot. It's as if the complete absence of shade gives the sun permission to just go nuts. Unlike his first two 100-milers, where we were stationary and Jason ran loops, this race is point to point, so we rented a minivan that would serve as a roving pit crew.

The logistics of the run were not that challenging, as it's hard to get lost going from island to island on massive bridges. The heat and humidity were difficult conditions for even the most seasoned ultra-runner. As someone who is warm all the time, the heat was particularly brutal for Jason. We saw other runners with bandannas that were filled with ice around their necks. We stopped at a gas station, bought a bandanna, and started making ice burritos for Jason's neck to try and keep him cool. It wasn't working like we needed it to. At mile 50, Jason bent over and started heaving up everything he had taken in, including his entire dinner, seemingly undigested from the night before. I had never seen anyone projectile vomit like that. Jimmy, Steve, and I stared at each other, silently wondering whether to call an ambulance or an exorcist. We had no clue about what to do. Jason felt a little better and wanted to keep going, so we continued to follow him, hoping he would be able to keep his nutrition down.

Not only was Jason unable to replenish what he threw up, he was also still throwing up everything he attempted to take in. Even water made him sick. Soon his run was a slow jog, then eventually a walk. I am not a mathematician, but it wasn't hard to figure out that at the pace he was moving, we were in for an extremely long night. We were 65 miles into the race and crewing him every mile. All three of us were taking turns pacing him, which was really walking with him to make sure he stayed awake. Jason was barely moving. I'm pretty sure I could have bunny hopped faster than he was walking. His body was completely shelled. The sun went down, and his pace slowed to a crawl. Jason started falling asleep. We tried talking to him, hoping that keeping him engaged would keep him awake. He wasn't able to drink Red Bull or anything else with caffeine that would normally help keep him awake. I am a really good at jabbering, and telling random stories is easy for me to do, but at the pace we were crawling, I ran out of things to say. I never thought I would get to a point in my life where I ran out of stories! So I started singing. Jason was so out of it that he couldn't protest anything at that point. Still falling asleep, but moving, I starting repeating, *Skidamarink a-dink, a-dink, Skidamarink a-doo, I love you!*

With every you I would squirt cold water on Jason's face. This kept him awake and aggravated. Relentless forward progress is a statement we say often. It doesn't matter how fast you are moving, as long as you are moving, and you're moving forward. We were barely moving, but we still moved forward, one inch at a time. We didn't keep track of how many times we opened and closed the minivan doors, but eventually we wore it out, and it stopped working.

The sun rose again. The light of the day brought heat, but it also brought some energy back for Jason. He was now able to tolerate very small amounts of liquids. He picked up his walk a bit faster. Jason really wanted to see the finish line. Steve yelled from the van, "You're almost there, Bro!" Jason replied, "I can't see it! Where is the finish?" The last two miles seemed to stretch out forever, but we finally made it to the finish line, almost 29 hours after starting. Steve, Jimmy, Jason, and I shared a finish line celebration. When your athlete has a bad race, it's hard for the crew, too. We were all so incredibly proud of Jason for his fortitude and continuing to push forward when anyone would have understood if he quit.

Steve, Jimmy, and I really wanted to go take pictures at the southern-most point of the United States. Jason, however, needed a wee bit of medical attention. EMSs were at the finish line and hooked him up to an IV of fluids. They hung the bag from the coat hook of the minivan, then left.

We really wanted to take these pictures, and since we were so close, it seemed like such an easy thing to just pop right over there before we headed back to the condo in Key Largo. Even though he had just fin-ished the most brutal 100 miles he would ever run, Jason was a good sport and agreed we would go take pictures. None of us had showered, but we didn't really care. When we got to the popular tourist spot, there was no place to park, and a long line of people were waiting. When you haven't slept in over 30 hours, funny things start happening. You have a tendency to not really care if things are socially appropriate or not.

"There's no place to park," decided Jimmy. "I am just going to leave the van here in the street. We will be quick."

We all climbed out of the van, and Jason started walking very gingerly toward the line. He still had the IV in his arm. Not wanting to ruin our great picture opportunity, he yanked the needle out and threw it away. The people in the line were staring at us. I am not sure if it was our smell or the fact that our ringleader pulled a needle out of his arm casually, but the line decided to part and let us go to the front.

Jason ended up developing a very serious case of rhabdomyolysis, a syndrome that is a result of the death of muscle fibers and the release of the protein myoglobin into the bloodstream. His kidneys were unable to process the waste, and he went into kidney failure. Hospitalized for several days was not how we anticipated his recovery would take place. Every event you participate in is a learning experience, regardless of the outcome. You process everything afterward, trying to figure out what you could do differently. People are understandably concerned about you when you race to the extreme point that you end up in the hospital. We both caught a lot of flak from people who thought we made a bad decision allowing Jason to continue on. As a crew, you have to assess every situation and each person and decide if they are harming themselves and what the risk to continue is. Jason didn't have any signs of rhabdo until over 24 hours after the race was over. Yes, we knew he was severely dehydrated but, no, we had no idea how bad it

was. If he had said to me at some point, wow…my pee looks like coffee, I would have gone on to the almighty Google and figured out what
in the world was going on.

Rhabdo takes a long time to recover from because, you know, parts
of your muscles have actually died. Jason felt a deep fatigue, even from
the lightest of workouts. It was really difficult for me to see him side-
lined, and I knew how much he hated not feeling well.

After crewing three 100-mile runs, it was easy to convince me that I
was never going to be an ultra-runner. I had an extreme amount of
respect for everyone that finished a 50-mile run, let alone 100! I was
also just really uninterested in running for that long. If Jason's race at
the Keys had been similar to his first or second 100-miler, I might have
had a different opinion. Watching the amount of suffering and torture
he put his body through was more than enough to convince me that I
was just not ready for that kind of event.

I was very curious about what it was like to work out for 24 hours. I
had learned that my body did okay crewing and pacing on very little
sleep. As long as I was doing something, it was easy to stay awake, but
crewing and racing are two very different things.

I started to research bike racing and if there were any events that I
could race in. Ultra-bike racing has a much smaller core group of athletes than ultra-running. Races exist, but they are infrequent. Racing in
the Southeast region is almost nonexistent.

My research lead me to a website called the UltraMarathon Cycling
Association, an international organization dedicated to the sport of

ultra-cycling. It was on this website that I discovered that you could set records for riding your bike in various states. It seemed simple enough. Someone sets a record for riding North-South, South-North, East-West, and West-East. Whoever is the first person to establish a record for the state gets to determine the starting and ending point. Then everyone else has to use the same points but gets to determine their own routes. You have rules to follow, and you have to bring an official who documents and records the record attempt. Seems simple enough, right?

I was nearing the five-year anniversary of breaking my leg. Florida was far from my first choice for a super-long bike ride. I perused each state, looking to see how long each record was and whether a woman had made an attempt or not. There were so many different distances to choose from. I knew I wanted something close enough to drive to, but also long enough that it would be at least 24 hours of riding.

In spite of everything, I settled on the state of Florida, from West to East. I joined the UltraMarathon Cycling Association, sent in my application and payment, and asked permission to attempt to set a record from the Georgia/Alabama State line to Neptune Beach, some 400+ miles away. They responded with an approval for my dates. Now I just needed to get a crew and an official, and submit my turn-by-turn directions.

My five-year accident anniversary was going to be spent becoming an ultra-cyclist right in the state where it all started. It was beginning to feel almost appropriate.

I am by no means an expert in love or relationships. I am, however, an expert in having fun. What is fun for me and what is fun for you might be different, but one thing remains the same: relationships are the most successful when you find someone you can have fun with. You might not share the same hobbies or passions with your partner, and this is okay; just remember, what makes them happy should make you happy.

We all have certain expectations, and when those are not met, we aren't happy. Do yourself a favor and don't assume your spouse or partner is a mind reader. If you want something tell them, and be specific.

My last piece of advice is to keep an open dialogue about things. Communication is key. Don't sign up for any crazy races, buy a sports car, or quit your job to backpack through Europe without having a clear and direct conversation about it. After all, this is a partnership, right? You should always want and need their blessing and support and be willing to give yours when it's needed.

PHOTOS

In Kentucky with my mother and brother, long before fitness was a priority.

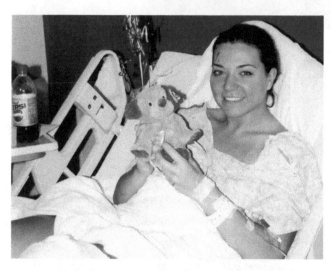

Recovering in a Florida hospital after surgery to repair my broken leg.

Trying to stay calm before my first ultra-cycling record attempt.

Embracing my #1 Crew Chief after a record-setting ride across Florida.

Jason and me before the Florida Anvil Triathlon.

Calling my dad after the Florida Anvil Triathlon, along with crew members, Emily and Jill.

Ready for a night on the town in Key West. This was after Jason's 12.5-mile swim around the island.

Keith chasing down a tossed bottle during RAAM.

Crew members, Keith, Beau, and Leslie start an impromptu dance to help keep spirits up.

Wedged among supplies during a sleep break on RAAM.

Celebrating with my dad in Annapolis, one of my most cherished moments in racing.

The entire Power, Pedals and Ponytail team—weary but elated in Annapolis.

Enjoying a local short-course race; going fast hurts!

Goofing off with Epic Ellie before the start of Epic 5.

Early on in Day 1, in Kauai.

Realizing the
rim is cracked
but trying to
stay cheerful.

With Chet "The Jet"
Blanton, super
pacer and friend.

Unexpected
flight issues
meant time to
catch up on
sleep.

**Attitude is everything! My bike
was broken, but not my spirit.**

Trying to stay cool on Day 5 in Kona.

WHAT ARE ULTRA-RACES ANYWAY?

Deciding to ride your bicycle across a state in an attempt to set a new record is like deciding to become a sport fishing captain. You know it will be challenging, but it's just fishing, right? But the part of your brain that keeps you from naively going into ventures that could easily get you killed is there for a very good reason. I needed a coach. The problem was that I didn't know many *ultra*-cyclists, and I definitely wasn't aware of anyone who had experience coaching them.

So I decided to hire someone I knew personally: an endlessly patient young sage of endurance, wrapped in a ridiculous amount of neon green Dri-FIT and spandex—Andrew *Snooches* Shanks. I knew him from his work at Dynamo Multisport, and I felt like he was smart enough to answer my questions, patient enough to deal with my stubbornness, and funny enough to know when I was giving him a hard time.

If I was going to be successful at my first attempt at ultra-cycling, I needed to start riding my bike, a lot. Shanks carefully crafted my workouts each week. The hardest adjustment for me was the sheer amount of time I needed to spend training each week. A three- to five-hour run is long, but three to five hours on the bike is nothing if you're into endurance sports. I used to think six-hour rides were long. Now I was doing eight- to ten-hour rides regularly. Just allotting time for workouts like these is almost impossible. And then there's the part where you are actually *riding* a bike for ten hours.

While I was busy pedaling each weekend, Jason was hard at work developing the route I would ride. UltraMarathon Cycling Association rules require that your starting and ending point be the same as the first person who set the record for the state. No rider is required to take the same route or even has access to other rider's routes. There was a 36-page rule packet with carefully outlined rules and regulations that needed to be followed in order for this to be a viable and safe record attempt. We were made aware that the current male record holder had a section of his route that was deemed unsafe due to bridge crossings. We were informed that we had to go around the bridge, riding a less direct but safer route. Also a longer route, as it turned out…

The great part about a record attempt is that you get to select and submit the date you want to ride. We chose early December in hopes the weather would be cooler. This would allow me a solid six months to prepare my body for the joys that come with riding a bike for over 24 hours.

While Jason was great at the logistics and planning for my attempt, he was getting restless post-rhabdo to start training for something. His friend Kellie had signed up for a race to be held in Hawaii that December called "Epicman," a triple-iron distance event that was the mutant brainchild of Jason Lester. Like any good ultra-friend, Kellie was calling Jason because she thought he should do the race, too.

"Hey, do you want to go to Hawaii for Christmas?" Jason asked.

"Of course! Sounds amazing! What's the catch?" I knew Jason better than to assume we would actually be traveling to Hawaii to *vacation.*

"There is a race, called Epicman. It's a triple Ironman." Jason replied.

"Oh, cool. Like a race a day, right?" I asked.

Jason looked at me and casually said, "No, like a triple; 421.8 miles of racing all at once."

I *should* have voiced concerns over the idea of swimming 7.2 miles in the ocean, a 336-mile bike ride, and a 78.6-mile run. But no one likes a party pooper, so I enthusiastically agreed to join Jason and crew for him in December.

I continued my training, diligently riding my bike week after week just as Coach Shanks prescribed. I was also swimming for recovery and doing weekly strength sessions along with a couple yoga sessions. The best part about the training was that I didn't have to ride alone; Jason was now on board for my 8- to 12-hour jaunts in the north Georgia mountains.

One day, I overheard Jason on the phone with Kellie. She must have been encouraging him to get me to sign up for Epicman, as she was the sole female in the event. I don't know exactly what Jason said, but it was something along the lines of *"Dani would never do anything like that."*

Oh, I *wouldn't,* would I? Jason has never, ever, said I *couldn't.* He is smart enough to know that I can do anything I want to do. He just noted that I wouldn't try an ultra-triathlon, which was a fair statement to make, considering that a 15-mile run was the max amount I was willing to endure. On the other hand, I once stopped eating meat for over six months because Jason bet me I couldn't. I eventually received a letter from Chick-Fil-A stating that their business model was unsustainable without my help. I couldn't stand the thought, so I went back to eating meat, but only after my six months were over and Jason had a realistic sense of my resolve.

By the time he hung up the phone, I had decided I was going to do an ultra-triathlon.

I signed up for the Florida Anvil triathlon to be held in February 2012. A double Ironman distance, it would consist of a 4.8-mile swim, a 224-mile bike, and a 52.4-mile run. In addition to biking a lot, I now needed to up my swim and run game. Shanks kept layering on more work. We decided to hold off on running any crazy distances until after the Florida state record was broken.

December approached much more quickly than I expected. My official route was set at 420 miles. I had a crew of Jason and Chuck, and my UMCA official was Keith. Signage was ordered for the van, amber lights and a red warning triangle purchased. I got my bike tuned up, clothes packed, nutrition plan written out, and was ready to go.

Shanks and I met for lunch a couple weeks before the trip to hash out the plan for my assault on the Florida panhandle.

"Alright, Shanks! What's the plan?" I was excited to hear what magical plan he had for me. "Okay. We'll hold X watts at Y heart rate for this amount of time, and when you get to EXACTLY the 92-mile mark, you will eat this many calories in the form of a fancy formula I have been working on with a team of Norwegian scientists, then up the power by Z percent for another very specific amount of time, after which we will have the theme from "Karate Kid" blaring out of loudspeakers on the van, and the blue angels will do a flyover, which will be your cue to..." You know, something like that.

"You ride. Eat. Ride. Eat." Shanks replied in a very nonsatisfying way.

"That's it?" I asked. "Just ride my bike?"

"Yep. Just ride. Nice and steady. And don't be a moron." Shanks knew me well enough to know I was not seasoned and easily excited. This can be a recipe for disaster at an event that requires incredible patience and pacing.

So that was my plan. Ride and eat like someone who isn't a moron. When I stopped, what I ate and when, where to turn—those were all important details but things I couldn't bother myself with. These were all things my crew could worry themselves with. Riding 420 miles in less than 27 hours and 58 minutes and eating was all I needed to do.

Because Florida West to East was a record a woman had not attempted before, I knew by simply finishing I would set the record. This was okay-ish. The truth was that I wanted to break the existing record of 405.3 miles in 27:58. Call me competitive, but I really needed a little carrot dangled in front of me to keep me motivated.

Jason, Chuck, Keith, and I traveled to the Florida/Alabama state line and checked into a cheap motel. We enjoyed a nice dinner together and all felt relaxed and at ease. I started getting anxious that night when I checked the weather. The forecast called for rain and wind.

All night I heard the wind. I repeated to myself, *it's a tailwind, it's a tailwind,* over and over. I woke up to a light drizzle and wind. We had planned to start at dawn, knowing it would be a long day and night. The ride start was uneventful, nothing official other than starting our watches. I felt like I should yell "honk" toward the heavens to signify the start, but Shanks had very recently reminded me not to be a moron.

Immediately I felt overdressed for the humid Florida weather. I peeled a layer off and handed it to my support van. The wind was unreal. Crosswinds and headwinds forced me to grip my bars harder than normal as I was alternately slowed and then driven sideways. Normally, I handle winds well, given that I am not a terribly *lightweight* person. Today was different; I felt like I was getting thrashed all over the roads.

We turned on Highway 98, and the winds worsened. I was using a small Motorola radio to communicate needs back to my support van. I radioed in:

"How much longer until my next turn?" I asked.

"A while," Jason radioed back.

"How long is a while?" Patience was wearing thin already.

"A hundred miles," Jason responded.

It was demoralizing to look at my bike computer and heart rate. *"Relentless forward progress,"* I told myself. *"Don't let yourself get in a negative space. You aren't riding 420 miles. You are riding four 105-mile rides...105 miles is nothing."*

One hundred ten miles in, and I started to get sleepy. I requested caffeine over the radio, which Jason promptly denied me, telling me it was too early in my ride. Ten miles later, the wind died down, and my energy levels picked up. We had large magnetic signs printed that said, *"Caution: Dani Cycling Ahead"* and *"Cross State Record Attempt in Progress."* People would drive by me hanging out their windows yelling, "GO, DANI, GO!" For such a simple gesture, it definitely changed the way I was feeling.

My crew continued radioing me directions and handing me nutrition from the van. We stopped at several gas stations for more fuel, and sometimes on the side of the road for wardrobe changes. At one stop, I noticed Jason using the bathroom in the bushes. It occurred to me that he was also making my sandwiches and not washing his hands!

Hand sanitizer...I had packed it all and forgotten hand sanitizer. Endurance sports are a lot of things, and one of those things is *gross*.

One hundred sixty miles in, I started to get a sharp pain in my left knee that I had never felt before. We stopped and applied some ice, massaging it gently. We had a cold laser with electrical stimulation that provided some relief as well.

Relentless forward progress.

The less I thought about the pain, the less apparent it became.

As the sun set and night came, I found myself riding through parts of Florida that were much hillier than I expected. Florida is the flattest state in the U.S., but Tallahassee didn't seem flat. The change in terrain was welcomed, and it allowed me to sit up some and get out of my aerobars.

My fluid intake was catching up with me, and I was now feeling the need to stop and pee every hour. One A.M., two A.M., three A.M., all came and went. Twenty-four-hour gas stations were plentiful, and I would dart in and out as quickly as possible in my neon reflective gear with safety lights still flashing.

The knee pain was still present, and Jason encouraged me to not grind, and to slow my cadence down. I asked him to talk to me over the radio to keep me awake and keep my mind off my knee. He read me Facebook and Twitter messages, emails, and texts from friends. We joked and laughed as much as possible. I tried to keep myself as happy as possible by reminding myself that this was fun! Is it really fun if you have to convince yourself that it is fun? The answer is *"mostly some-times yes and no."*

Before I knew it, I was 300 miles into the ride. My riding pace was good, and I was set to break the record, despite having to ride an additional 15 miles. I was trying to make my pit stops as fast as possible, but I felt like I had to stop every 45 minutes to pee.

With less than 100 miles to go, I decided I was going to stop one last time then just hold it. This was getting ridiculous. It was probably just

nerves anyway, right? I pulled over and ran into some bushes. Hurriedly I pulled down my bike shorts, did my business, and pulled them back up, only to discover I hadn't quite pulled them down far enough. I had just peed on my shorts.

As the great Chuck Mathison would say, "The thing about it is, you have to be comfortable being uncomfortable." I think he was talking about this exact situation, because I was about to get a big lesson in discomfort.

The last 80 miles went by really fast. The route Jason planned was around 417 miles, but we knew that it might end up being a tad longer. The closer we got to 417 miles, the more anxious I started to get about breaking the record. It was going to be close.

When we hit 417 miles, I was mentally done. I was riding parallel to the ocean and knew that my ending point was Neptune Beach. There was construction, and roads were closed. I could hear the waves, I could smell the beach, I could even *see* the beach, but I couldn't quite get there.

At 420 miles, I got really angry.

"WHERE IS THE BEACH?!" I screamed into the headset. "I'D BETTER SEE SOME DAMN DOLPHINS, TOO!"

Jason kept telling me to hold on, he needed to check a map. I was on the verge of losing my mind; 27 hours and 49 minutes had passed. If I didn't find the beach soon I was really going to go crazy.

Still no beach after 421 miles. I was frantic at this point and riding like a maniac. The follow van was carefully stopping at stop signs while I was barely pausing.

Finally, that glorious damned beach! My bike computer said 422 miles despite the fact that our *official* Google Maps mileage had the route at 420. At 27 hours, 54 minutes, I made it.

I literally ran to the beach. Jason was hugged me telling me how proud he was of me. Chuck was taking pictures, and Keith was writing notes, diligently documenting everything for the UMCA. I was in total shock; *had I really ridden my bike for almost 28 hours?*

I found the closest bathroom I could, ditched my bike shorts, changed into clean clothes, and hopped in the van. With no time to waste, we were back on the road, headed to Atlanta.

IF ONE IRONMAN IS FUN, TWO SHOULD BE DOUBLE FUN...RIGHT?

My body healed quickly from the ride across Florida—with the exception of my right arm. I had spent so much time with a death drip on my aerobars that I had developed a painful case of de Quervain's tenosynovitis, which caused me to spend several days without the use of my thumb, and a couple weeks in a wrist brace. When I moved my wrist, you could hear the tendon sheaths squeaking. Writing and typing were painful for several months, as was riding my road bike and pulling my arm through the water when I swam.

This was a problem, because I needed to switch gears and start training for the Florida Double Anvil. It became apparent that the bigger you go, the more risk you have of getting injured, so I enlisted the help of local massage therapist and accomplished ultra-athlete, Eileen Steil, to get me back on track.

Within a couple of weeks, my arm was healed up enough for me to rejoin my masters swimming group. I had approximately eight weeks before it was time for my 281.2-mile jaunt.

There was one other thing going on in December—*Epicman*. My excitement grew with each day. On Christmas Eve, Jason gave me the most thoughtful gift: a silver necklace with *422* engraved on it, flanked by two purple amethysts—a beautiful reminder of my cross-state journey.

We flew to Oahu on Christmas morning. Hawaii is pretty much everything everyone says it is. It is just beautiful. Even the air smells like the Chamber of Commerce is pumping some kind of mind control perfume into it. In the days leading up to the event, I ran in parks and swam in the ocean. We met local celebrity athlete Chet Blanton, who has raced more than any human I have ever met, and he loaned me his road bike to get my training in.

Epicman was conceived (probably in a dark basement laboratory) by Jason Lester, an extremely seasoned ultra-athlete and Hawaii resident. The event would start off with a 7.2-mile swim in Ala Moana State Park, a 112-mile ride around Oahu, then a 224-mile ride on a closed course and three marathons. Athletes would finish in Kapiolani Park, and they had 60 hours to complete the event.

Each athlete was required to bring their own support, and local volunteers supplemented each athlete's crew. Jason was the only athlete with just one crew member—me. At the pre-race meeting, I started getting nervous. We were finding that driving in Oahu wasn't easy; the 13-letter Hawaiian alphabet meant that three different roads had names like *Ahi St., Ahihi St.*, and *Ahiahi St.* Not confusing at all, especially if you are mentally fatigued. I did find some amusement in the fact that there was a street called *Aholehole St.* It's the little things. My driving skills are questionable on the easiest roads, so I was very thankful when I learned a local volunteer was going to drive me in the van for the 112-mile ride around the island.

I made the assumption that I would be using a kayak to support Jason on the swim. Imagine my surprise when, on race morning, they gave me a stand-up paddle board, or SUP. I thought this would have been good info to have a few months prior, as I had never been on a SUP before in my life.

Jason blew the swim away, and I tried to keep up with him for 7.8 miles on the SUP without tipping over. I won't lie; I definitely sat down and took a break. Your first time on a stand-up paddle board should not be a three-hour trip in the ocean.

The 112-mile ride around the island was the original Ironman Hawaii World Championship course before the event was moved to Kona. My local guide and driver, Dave, was incredible. Not only did he know the course like the back of his hand, but he also had pieces of local history that he sprinkled in along the way.

With only five athletes participating in Epicman, it was a very cozy event. The bike course proved to be worthy of a world championship race—it was hot, hilly, windy, and incredibly scenic. Jason rode through the pineapple fields and was feeling great.

By nightfall, the athletes were beginning to feel the accumulation of the 14+ hours of racing. Around 200 miles into the bike, Jason pulled over and started throwing up. Fearing another repeat from the Keys, I made him start peeing into Dixie cups to check the color of his urine.

Not being able to keep nutrition down slowed Jason's pace, but he continued to ride. I made him pee in the Dixie cups anytime he stopped. Watching for signs of rhabdo, I felt confident he was okay to continue.

Relentless forward progress. Jason ticked the miles away. The sun rose again, and Jason began his second full day of racing. The sun brought back the heat, but it also woke up the three athletes who remained.

Jason Lester ran the first marathon with Jason. There was no way I could pace him for 78 miles in addition to being a caretaker and driving the van. I had tried to sleep the night before, but knowing Jason was struggling left me unable to do so.

As the day wore on, Jason's stomach started to settle. His run pace was exactly what you would expect after swimming 7.2 miles and a 336-mile bike ride. This was going to be a long day. The sun set again, and Jason was still walk/jogging. Sleep deprivation was setting in.

Jason had given me strict instructions not to allow him to sleep, but his body wasn't cooperating. He would pause for a *minute* to sit in the back of van only to pass out. I would fall asleep, too, and Jason would wake up 20 to 30 minutes later with his legs in fits, cramping from the sudden stopping.

Before athletes reached the finish, they had to run up Diamond Head, an inactive volcano crater and popular tourist spot. Jason's face was distorted from the pain, and with every step, he would yell out "ouch!" "dammit!" Busloads of tourists were staring at this seemingly insane man yelling curse words.

At this point, the sleep deprivation was taking a toll on me. We were closing in on 48 hours of racing, and I had slept less than two hours total. I started to get really emotional, which led to me crying uncontrollably at the pain Jason was in. I had no idea what to do to make him feel better. I called his brother, Steve.

"Sttteeeevvveeee!!!!" I wailed into the phone. "Jason's in sooooo much pain!" This was definitely the first time Steve had ever heard me cry.

"What kind of pain?" Steve asked.

"His hip hurts, and he's just hurting all over!" I replied between sobs.

"So he's going to finish, right? And you don't think you'll have to take him to the hospital, will you?" Steve was slowly bringing me back to reality.

"No, he won't have to go to the hospital." I wasn't crying anymore.

"Then stop crying, he's fine." Steve's lack of empathy was nothing new; he just knew his brother.

Steve was right. Jason *was* fine. He crossed the finish line at 49 hours and some change. After getting a full night's sleep, we went snorkeling, sky diving over the North Shore, hiking, and even made a shark tank expedition.

When we got back to Atlanta, Jason decided he would race the Florida Anvil as well. We had less than ten weeks to go. My fitness level was high from the ride across Florida, but I was lacking in running volume. I started hitting the pavement. Thanks to the diligent work of my masters coach, Maria, my swim was the strongest it had ever been.

A local friend asked me if I knew that there was another female from Atlanta racing in Florida. In an event with six total female participants, I was surprised to learn that one was from Atlanta and only lived 15 minutes away from us! I met up with Kacie Darden for a 20-mile run, and we chatted the entire time about life and racing. It was great to connect with another female in the community.

That 20-mile run would be my last run, as my Achilles decided to fight back with a horrible case of tendinitis. My worst fear about ramping up my run volume had come true. Biking was incredibly painful as well. I swam as much as I could and tried every type of therapy known to man to *heal my heel* before the race.

We traveled to Tampa, Florida, in late February with our crew, which consisted of our friends Jill, Emily, and, of course, Keith. Once the swim was over and we made our way to Flatwoods Park, the race would be stationary, so we figured it would be easy for a team of three to handle both Jason and me.

The Florida Anvil had 33 participants, with people traveling from as far Germany and Switzerland. We were required to check in two days early and get our fingers pricked and blood tested. This was a small event, but they took their doping seriously!

We started the race on a Friday, swimming 4.8 miles in a beautiful outdoor pool at the YMCA. We were all seeded based on expected swim times. I was in lane two, and Jason was in lane one. Being the only female in the lane, the guys were nice enough to let me start first. Within 600 meters, they were clamoring all over me. *Guys, we have a long day to be getting this competitive this early.* A couple thousand meters later, I was lapping people. I could see Jason swimming in the lane next to me, and he was having an awesome swim.

He got out of the water in 1:48, and I was behind him as the third person out, in 2:23.

As I mentioned before, I am terrible at directions. As much as I tried to pay attention to the way we were supposed to ride our bikes from the YMCA to Flatwoods Park (it was less than five miles), the truth was I couldn't remember anything. Add in the fact I had just swum 4.8 miles, and my brain was entirely focused on my pacing and racing, not trying to find a park. Not surprisingly, I found myself lost within the first couple miles. Thankfully, another racer, Ben, stumbled upon me. At 20, he was the baby of the race, and we found our way to Flatwoods Park together.

It was now time to activate my inner ultra-gerbil. We were riding a looped course—6.68-mile loops to be exact. If you think this is mentally excruciating, you're right. It's also the safest way to keep a small event managed when racers are separated by as much as ten hours at the finish. February races aren't easy, because it means you've likely been relegated to the trainer quite a bit over the winter. We were lucky; the South had been experiencing a very warm winter. Too bad the heat continued and found its way to us in Tampa. High 70s were much hotter than most racers were used to, and people were fading fast.

I was pacing myself and just doing my thing. Riding consistently is what I do, and today was no exception. I loved seeing my crew so often, and they would yell words of encouragement while handing me bottles or sandwiches. I was asking about Jason, and no one was giving me a really clear answer, so I knew something was up. A couple laps later, I passed him. Contrary to popular belief, we aren't competitive with each other. If I am ahead of him, it means that he isn't racing well, and I take no joy in knowing he doesn't feel good.

Jason took a break to cool off from the heat, which was exactly what he needed. He got back on the bike and rode strong, regaining his lead over me. By mile 180, it was dark out, and I was holding steady as the first-place female and third overall. Jason was second overall and not too far ahead of me.

Flatwoods Park is completely unlit at night. My night vision is less than optimal, and I was halfway through my last lap when my headlight started dimming. *"Wonderful,"* I thought. *"I am about to be riding com-*

pletely in the dark." I saw a blinking red light ahead of me. Another rider! I quickly caught up to Ben, my buddy from the beginning of the ride.

"Hey, Ben! My light is dead! Can I ride next to you?" I asked.

Ben adjusted his light so we could both see and led me in to my 31st and final lap. Emily and Jill helped me fumble around in the dark, doing a complete wardrobe change into running gear. Nothing is harder than putting clothes on when you are damp, and when you're soaked with sweat and almost delirious with fatigue, it's nearly impossible. My Achilles had been playing nice up until this point, but I was acutely aware that I was about to *run* 52.4 miles. I tried to ignore the fact that I was injured and had not run in six weeks.

The run course was similar to the bike—a ton of little loops, barely two miles each. An out and back, this meant we would be seeing a lot of the other racers. Nighttime running is one of my favorite things to do, partially because you aren't paying attention to your watch and how slow you're going, and mostly because there are lots of cool noises coming from the woods at night.

It didn't take long before my *run* was merely a jog that turned into a *walk/jog*. It was going to be a long night. Fifteen or so miles in, a female, who took the lead, passed me. She was running strong, and I knew there was no way that I could catch her. Keith, Emily, and Jill took turns running with me at night. They did their best to keep me moving as fast possible. Emily and I argued over whether I was actually walking or jogging.

"Okay, I am going to jog, and you walk, and we will see who is moving faster." I told her.

Emily walked, I jogged, and I was right. My slow jog *was* faster than her walk. We shuffled along.

It was getting harder and harder to take in nutrition, mostly because nothing was really palatable to me at that point. I nibbled on plain bread and flat Mountain Dew. The sun started to rise, and I found myself passing through the timing mat and seeing Jason sitting in a folding chair. *What's he doing?* I thought.

"Hey, babe! Whatcha doing?" I asked him.

"Just taking a little break," he responded.

"I think I am ahead of you now," I prodded him jokingly.

That was all he needed to hear. Jason took off, passing me on the next lap. The female who passed me early on had passed him as well, so Jason was sitting in third overall, and I was fourth. I was getting tired. This was the first race I had ever done where someone was pacing me, and I quickly discovered that I liked hearing stories. I wanted to focus on something, anything, other than the signals my body was giving me.

Keith is a man of few words. I was moving the fastest when I was with him, but I wanted stories. I tried to give him story ideas, even asking him to recount every animal he had ever owned—still nothing. He was laser focused on the race, and wanted me to be, too.

"Kacie is gaining on you," Keith told me.

"That's fine," I said. "She deserves to beat me. She trained a lot harder than I did." We had less than ten miles to go. I was giving up.

Keith cocked his head and gave me a sideways look. "That is *not* how we race."

He was right—Relentless. Forward. Progress.

I picked it up. Jason was right ahead of me, Kacie on my heels. I was ready to be done.

We were given a flag to cross the finish line with. Kirby, the race director, played the national anthem, and I collapsed into Jason's arms, tears of joy (and a touch of pain) rolling down my cheeks.

That was difficult. *Satisfyingly difficult.*

Out of 33 racers, 25 finished. Jason was second overall, and I was fourth. Six out of the 25 athletes were females, and all of the females who started, finished. Three out of the six females placed in the top five *overall* of the race. I was starting to learn that the longer the event, the more it equalized genders. This was a new way of racing, and I liked it.

Becoming part of the Dynamo Multisport family was one of the best decisions I have ever made as it relates to athletic performance. I started swimming masters at Dynamo pool. The moment you walk into the place, you can tell it's special. Thousands of swimmers have passed through there through the years. Countless hours and millions of yards have been swum by everyone from small children to recreational adults. Instead of an overchlorinated, overly hot pool, I was now swimming in a pristine pool with the faint smell of desire to succeed. You don't always know what you are missing. We are all motivated differently. Some of us need to run with groups or swim at masters for extra motivation. Other people are fine doing all of their workouts solo.

If you find yourself in a training slump, try checking out something different. Whether it's a local run club, a masters swim group, or a ride hosted from a bike shop, switching things up might be exactly what your body and mind are looking for!

6

RACE ACROSS AMERICA

*Courage, sacrifice, determination, commitment, toughness,
heart, talent, guts. That's what little girls are made of; the
heck with sugar and spice.*

—Bethany Hamilton

Race Across America was not even a blip on my radar until someone invited me to participate in an eight-person team in 2012. RAAM is a 3000-mile bike race from Oceanside, California, to Annapolis, Maryland. The race boasts that it's "not a stage race," meaning that once the clock starts, the time is ticking. With over 170,000 vertical feet of climbing and 12 different states to cross, the terrain is ever changing. You can race as an individual, with 12 days to complete the event or as an 8, 4, or 2-person team. All teams receive nine days to complete the race, regardless of size.

I knew that an eight-person team wasn't going to be enough riding for me to warrant taking that much vacation time, but I instantly thought about my new friend, Kacie, a schoolteacher with summers off.

Kacie participated in the eight-person team, and I became fascinated with the race and logistics. I tracked her, along with the soloist, all across the country. Shortly after she returned, Kacie called to tell me about her adventure.

What I remember about our conversation is mostly about the scenery; Monument Valley at sunrise, descending the Glass Elevator, the winds in Kansas. Then Kacie said the words I had not known I wanted to hear so badly: "We could do this race. We could do it as a two-person team. I think we would be really fast, and we could break the record." *I was instantly and completely on board.*

At that point, only two two-person female teams had completed RAAM within the time limits. The race is strongly male dominated, with only 18 percent of the field represented by women. I was a strong climber, and Kacie was a fearless descender. We both had the genetics for it; steady and strong, made for distance riding. We knew we would make a great team, but no race team will ever be successful without an even stronger crew.

I discussed RAAM with Jason, and Kacie got the blessing from her husband, George. They would start working on logistics while Kacie and I would start training and building our crew.

Most importantly, of course, was coming up with a cool team name and even better logo. We tossed around some options, and eventually **Power, Pedals, and Ponytails** was born. A friend of a friend in graphic design school created a cool logo of a bike cog with a pink and purple ponytail intertwined.

Since this was a different kind of race for me, I started working with a coach who had more experience in the ultra-arena, Heather Jones-

Proctor. Although she specialized in ultra-running and ultra-triathlon, Heather was extremely excited about the idea of Race Across America.

Kacie and I both started researching RAAM, ways to train, and problems people deal with. The internet had a lot of resources for us. We made arrangements to meet with anyone and everyone that had ever crewed or participated in RAAM in any capacity. The key to success was to plan for 1000 different things and then not have a meltdown when something happens that nobody could have expected. The dreaded, *thing number 1001.*

Heather's plan for me was simple. I was going to ride. Ride long, ride short, practice taking time off and on the bike. Focus on core work and continue swimming for recovery. We had about ten months to get ready.

I signed up for a 12-hour bike race in Texas that fall as a training race. It was complete and total misery. The roads were chip sealed. (This is basically a band-aid solution for failing road surfaces where tar and gravel are put down to seal the surface. The result is a bumpy, fatiguing mess.) It was hilly, and it poured rain the entire day. Because timed events are judged based on how many miles you've ridden within the 12 hours, you can quit anytime you want to, which for the second-to-last woman in the race was nine hours. As easy as it would have been to stop at 9 hours and 15 minutes, the competitive part of me came with the intent of riding for 12 hours. The practical side of me wanted to get her money's worth. It poured rain from start to finish, raining so hard I could barely see at times.

I spent several hours thinking about every time anyone I knew had quit something, and how that made me feel. It worked. I set the course record, riding 211.22 miles, and came in second place overall. Jason raced in the 500-mile event, winning it, and coming within 17 minutes of breaking the course record.

I spent the winter practicing riding off and on. I would spend all day on my trainer, riding for 30 minutes to an hour, then taking a 30-minute break, and then back on the trainer. When the weather was above 35°, I would ride outside.

As my training got progressively longer, my ability to pitch in at home declined. I would teach a bike class on Tuesday evenings. Leaving work at 5:00, I could ride from 5:30 P.M. to 8:00 P.M. I'd get home around 8:45 P.M. and needed to get up at 4:30 A.M. to ride again. On more than one occasion, I asked Jason if I *really* had to shower, since technically all I was doing was getting up and riding again. (Practicing lowered levels of personal hygiene is good ultra-training—if I haven't mentioned it before, this sport can be outright gross.) Jason would force me to eat and shower. At 4:30 A.M., if my feet weren't on the floor in 30 seconds, Jason would start saying, "RAAM! RAAM! RAAM!" until I got up. There is no lack of support or motivation in this house.

Your crew is possibly the second most important asset you have in a race, next to your health. The same is true during training—your roommate, significant other, parents, whomever you spend the lion's share of your time with, becomes your crew while you train. No matter which of us is training for what event, we are both 100 percent goal focused. I'm sure it could be done without this kind of support, but it would be exponentially more difficult.

Kacie and I started working on finding a crew. Have you ever tried to get a group of friends just to agree on an evening to go out and have dinner? Even more difficult, a weekend to go to the beach or whatever? It's practically impossible. *Now consider that we would be asking friends to basically be miserable for eight to nine days, and we can't pay them. So burn up your vacation for the year because you love us. Oh, and there won't be much sleeping. Or eating. And almost no bathing. And you'll be in a van for most of it.* So in the aforementioned going out to dinner scenario, you know how you have that one friend who wants to split the bill all weird because *he only had one bite of the appetizer and his wine was cheaper than the other wine?* Yeah, that guy is definitely staying the hell home and needs to stop being invited to anything ever, anyway. This is not an endeavor where we have time to split hairs or cater to your high maintenance needs. And the other friend you have, whom you love dearly but is perpetually ten minutes late to everything? She can't go either. We had to find people who could make the sacrifice, be insanely flexible, stay focused, and maintain their general good nature and sanity through some pretty severe sleep deprivation. Luckily, we already had a few who were just exactly that awesome/crazy. Those words are fairly interchangeable in this context.

Jason and George were in. Jason's brother, Steve, was also in, and of course so was Keith. Kacie's close friend, Anne, and her coach, Will, were also on board. Emily, who crewed for us at the double and is a bike mechanic, wanted in on the action. We had a solid crew of seven but knew that we needed more. Kacie had someone who had crewed for her eight-person team: Leslie, with extensive experience, as she had crewed a two-person team as well. We were left looking for several more people.

One day, I got a call from Ben, my buddy from the double who guided me in when my light died. Ben was in town visiting his grandfather and wanted to get together. It turned out he had just graduated college and had the entire summer off before going to medical school. Oh, how I was about to make him regret divulging that bit of information. Actually, I knew he'd be perfect for RAAM and he'd love it. I casually mentioned that, since he was not doing much this summer, he should hang out with Kacie and me for a couple weeks. And by hang out, I mean watch us from a van going 15-mph for 3,000 miles. Ben thought it sounded awesome. I knew I liked that kid!

I received a Facebook message one day from a guy named Beau whom I knew loosely from the triathlon community. Keith had run into him and told him that he was crewing RAAM. Keith had called me, telling me that Beau wanted in on the adventure. I was surprised that he was so excited. Being the straight shooter that I am, I wanted to make sure that he was well aware that RAAM was not going to be a party across the country.

This was my sales pitch to Beau : "You won't shower much, or at all. You will be in tight quarters with people you don't know well, but you are required to get along with them. There are going to be very limited options for what you will eat. You will need to drive, or possibly navigate, or maybe be a domestique. Your mission is to get us from Oceanside to Annapolis safely, without breaking rules. It'll be a lot like that TV show where everybody is forced to live together, only without the personality disorders and showering together, or showering at all. Oh, yeah, and we want to break the record."

No pressure or anything.

Beau was totally in. Our last addition was a massage therapist from Iowa, whom neither of us had even met, named Kim.

Unless your crew has crewed together, it is highly advisable to spend time together. Not just to get to know each other, but to see who works best with whom. We did a crew retreat, carefully outlining our expectations and allowing the crew some time to display their strengths and weaknesses. Kacie and I had different personalities, and our needs were not the same. It was important to us that we were careful about picking out the best choices for our individual crews and the team as a whole.

Race Across America has a long list of rules, mostly designed for safety of the rider and crew. A *race simulation* was on our calendar that spring to break in people who had no crew experience. Driving behind a rider at night, navigating, racking and reracking bikes, all sound simple in theory, but at some point, fatigue would require some degree of muscle memory to ensure as few mistakes as possible.

Kacie and I started our 24-hour race simulation with a 12-hour ride together. Around 7:00 P.M., the local crew met up with us. We set up two follow vehicles and asked our crew to follow RAAM rules. We took turns riding 30 minutes on and 30 minutes off. Twelve hours each and a *scrillion* shift changes later, we had completed our 24-hour ride. Our crew did a beautiful job navigating the country roads of northwest Georgia.

We only had one other *practice* scenario—a 535-ish-mile (really, once you are over a hundred or so, who cares?) bike race in rural Alabama called Heart of the South. The course was grueling; we started at night, and it was cold and extremely hilly. Sometimes the best training races are the ones were you can find yourself getting tested mentally and physically, and Heart of the South definitely did that for us.

The logistics for an event of the magnitude of RAAM are overwhelming. Jason, George, and Anne each took a share of the work. Kacie and I continued to train while fundraising for Camp Twin Lakes, a local nonprofit organization that provides camp experiences to Georgia children with disabilities, serious illnesses, or other life challenges. Fundraising events combined with travel arrangements for 13 people and race logistics will wear even the most energetic person out. This was turning out to be a lot more complicated than *just riding your bikes across the country*, but we were almost there.

WELCOME TO OCEANSIDE

Oceanside, California, was taken over by Race Across America. You could feel the energy in the air. About 50 percent of the race is composed of crews and athletes from outside the U.S. While not everyone speaks the same language, we all share in our love of all things related to bicycles!

In the days prior to the race, Kacie and I tried to maintain a low profile. We were invited to participate in a panel discussion and an interview, but other than that, we let our crew do most of the work related to getting us race ready. There was a mandatory crew meeting and an inspection of all the race vehicles and equipment. We tried to remain off our feet as much as possible. The crew dealt with all the details around inspection, and shielding us from as much pre-race anxiety as possible.

When your race is going to last longer than a week, there is not a big rush to start first thing in the morning. The race didn't start until noon, giving athletes and crew the opportunity to get a good night's rest and a full meal. I showered and washed my hair, not knowing if I would have the chance to bathe again before Annapolis. We headed to a local breakfast spot and got acai bowls. I felt incredibly calm, considering what we were about to undertake.

Kacie and I each had our own minivans that were outfitted with our own clothing and food. Our plan was to ride for around 30 minutes off and on during the daytime hours (7:00 A.M. to 7:00 P.M. local time) and leapfrog each other. We were each going to take a one-hour break during the day while the other person rode. Our nighttime game plan was to each ride a four-hour pull while the other person ate a large meal and slept as long as she could.

Each rider had a three-person crew during the day in their van. The crew's roles were driver, navigator, or caretaker. From 7:00 P.M. to 7:00 A.M. local time, the crew vans were required to do direct follow, which meant that they had to be behind the rider at all times. Each van was given a thick route book, the *Bible of RAAM*, that listed turn-by-turn directions. I had a two-person crew at night and, since we had an odd number of crew, Kacie had three.

There are 52 time stations in Race Across America. Each team has to call in to race headquarters when they reach the time station and report the time they arrived. Sometime the stations are manned with actual volunteers, but most are just gas stations or empty parking lots.

The first 24 miles of the race are unsupported, which means your crew vans cannot access you at all. Generally, teams will send two people to ride this section so, if someone has a mechanical issue, the other person can continue riding. Since two was all our team was composed of, we decided we would both ride that section.

The start line of RAAM was one of the coolest things I've ever seen. A huge banner hung above the start line, and large crowd formed on the street adjacent to the beach. It is customary for riders to dip their bike wheel in the Pacific Ocean, signifying that they started as far west as they could have.

Although it's a race, RAAM does not have a mass-start. Each rider and team takes off on their own after being announced by the race officials. Kacie and I lined up waiting for our turn. I looked down at her watch and saw her heart rate was really high.

"Are you okay?" I asked.

"Yeah, I'm good." Kacie replied. "I think I am starting to get nervous."

It was understandable, considering the amount of pressure on us. We had 11 people who were making a huge sacrifice to help us break a record, on top of all the support our friends, family, and community had given us back home. While we had done a really good job of keeping these pressures balanced with what we described as *the ministry of fun,*" we both felt the pressure. Months of training were now coming down to what we would be capable of doing in the next eight to nine days.

Our names were announced as the only two-person female team participating in RAAM that year. We took off and rode the first 24 miles together, climbing inland towards Palomar Mountain. We started leapfrogging each other as we continued to climb. Wearing Cardo radios in our ears, our vehicles told us which turns to make. We could radio back if we had issues or needed something.

Kacie descended the *Glass Elevator,* a gorgeous and dangerous descent that brought us into Borrego Springs. Near the Salton Sea, we were now in the desert. Only 140 miles into the race, and the temperatures had changed dramatically. We were continuing to head south; in fact, we were less than 20 miles from Mexico. Our route book warned us that there was limited cell service as we headed toward Arizona, and if you needed supplies for the next 150 miles, you'd better stop at the Walmart once you got there.

Everyone tells you that no one sleeps the first night of RAAM, and they are right. You're too excited and wound up to get any good rest. Because the race started at noon, we just weren't physically tired, either.

Day two saw us heading into harder climbing in Arizona. It was getting hot. We were riding really well and continued to keep up with four-person male and mixed teams. This was great for our psyche and extremely motivating. I am not sure that the other riders appreciated seeing us out there with them, but we didn't care.

Our crew was doing a wonderful job, so far, of keeping us on course, fed, and in good spirits. Sticking to our plan, each rider was taking a two-hour pull late in the afternoon. Part of my pull that afternoon was a 12-mile climb, ending at 7000 feet. Pacing and strategy were super important, but let's face it—passing people is really fun. I saw two guys from a four-person team. I tried to hold back—really I did—but I couldn't help it. I passed them, steadily turning my pedals over. After my descent through the adorable town of Jerome, it was time for me to take my one-hour break. The problem was that we were in the desert, and it was really freaking hot.

I plopped into the back of our *sleeper* van, which was really just an 18-passenger van with the rear seats removed and a twin mattress in their place. Some teams had the luxury of renting RVs for sleep, but we just didn't have that kind of money. Fearing that the vans would over-heat in the desert if left running idle, Kacie and I tried to sleep in the vans, parked in the shade. We were quickly realizing that our plans of taking a one-hour nap during the day were unsuccessful.

We left Arizona and made our way into Utah.

There was an eight-person male team from Germany that we had been exchanging places with throughout the night, and I had caught one of their riders again as we entered Mexican Hat, Utah.

In his thick German accent, he said, "You women are very strong. You keep catching us."

"Yeah we are pretty strong...for women," I joked.

He replied, "Vvvelllll, ve are old. But zere are eight of us, aannnddd only two of you."

He picked up the pace and took off. Moments later, wild horses started galloping next to me. I started shrieking into the radio.

"Horses! Someone's horses are loose!"

"Those horses are wild!" Steve replied.

It was such a beautiful site, wild horses galloping next to the most beautiful red rock formations.

"I wonder what they eat," I questioned.

"Cyclists who aren't riding fast enough!" Steve laughed into the radio.

I liked Utah a lot, but every state we marked off the list meant we were closer to Maryland.

Colorado was up next. We were almost 800 miles into the race, and while we were sleeping better at night, our crew was starting to realize that the four-hour pulls were just a little bit too long for us to be riding at an optimal speed.

We headed into the Colorado Rockies and picked up crew member Leslie in Durango, Colorado. Although I am sure it was planned out, it was as if she just materialized on the side of the road with four large pizzas.

Jason opened up the pizza box and looked at it disgustedly. "Vegetables! This friggin' pizza is COVERED in vegetables! I can't eat this!"

Emily chimed in, "UGH. I don't want it, either!"

Kacie is a vegetarian, and I wondered if our pizzas had been swapped. *Man, I hope she isn't so desperate for food that she eats sausage. "What happens to vegetarians when they eat meat? Do they explode?"* I thought as I ate the pizza. We had already been warned that food was hard to come by, so we ate what we could when we could.

The altitude continued to rise as we made our way into the Rockies. We were warned to be on the lookout for elk and deer, especially at night.

Kacie and I had discussed a couple of things about the course specifically, and I was not fond of the idea of descending at night. I am legally blind in my left eye. This makes me a horrible driver with bad depth perception. My night vision leaves a lot to be desired.

We had 45 miles and 6,548 feet of climbing ahead of us to the top of Wolf Creek Pass. The sun was going down. At 7,000 feet elevation, Kacie was starting to experience some altitude sickness and wasn't feeling good. If you haven't raced at altitude, it's hard to describe—I once heard someone say, "It's like a normal ride, but with a pair of socks stuffed in your mouth." The air is thin, so there's just not enough of it. Some people getting splitting headaches, some get nauseated and start throwing up. Many people suddenly get very fatigued and feel light-headed.

As we gained elevation, Kacie's condition worsened. We started the climb up Wolf Creek Pass, and I realized I was going to have to descend it completely in the dark. It was the only thing I didn't want to do during the race. When we got to the top, where the elevation peaked at 10,856 feet, I saw Kacie collapse in the back of her van, helmet and shoes still on.

Anne came up to me. "There was an incident with a deer on this descent," she said. Just the kind of news I didn't want to hear.

"What kind of incident?" I asked as I was adding layers of clothes on.

"A rider got hit and broke his leg," Anne replied.

Anne's solution for this was to ride behind me, hanging out the window and ringing a cowbell. She yelled, too, which might have been to scare off the deer or keep me awake, because I was barely able to keep my eyes open.

My teeth were chattering as I started down the mountain. I pulled over several times for more clothes, Mountain Dew, gels—really, anything to give myself a brief break. I was so nervous yet so tired at the same time. I grew increasingly frustrated at myself because I knew I wasn't descending fast.

Relentless forward progress. I told myself. *I barely have to pedal here. Just keep moving…*

At some point, our crew realized that our initial plan for rider pulls wasn't working. The four-hour breaks at night were just a little too long. We were waking up early, and the other rider was slowing down. A new game plan was formulated. It was decided that we would continue the 30- minute pulls during the day but ditch the 1-hour break. From 7:00 P.M. to 7:00 A.M., we would now take three-hour pulls and alternate that with a three-hour break, twice. I would ride from 7:00 P.M. to 10:00 P.M., Kacie from 10:00 P.M. to 1:00 A.M., me again from 1:00 A.M. to 4:00 A.M., and Kacie from 4:00 A.M. to 7:00 A.M. The hope was that during this three-hour break we would change out of our cycling kits, eat a full meal, and get at least two hours of sleep. The other rider should ride faster if they were doing a three-hour pull instead of four. Some shifting of crew was done as well. We now had a daytime and nighttime crew, and they did 12-hour shifts.

Colorado is absolutely stunning in the summertime. The mountains were still snow capped as we continued to ride farther and farther away from civilization. The teams were now getting more spread apart. We would go hours without seeing anyone else riding on the roads from the race.

As we headed toward the plains, Kacie started to feel better. We were 1,200 miles into the race, and our crew was doing an amazing job of keeping us on track to break the record. My daytime crew of Beau, Keith, and Leslie were passing the time by having dance contests on the side of the road as we waited to see Kacie and her crew. The guys were trying to do push-ups for every mile, and falling short.

The plains of Colorado were a wonderful change from the climbing that had taken us several days. We were approaching time station #23 and had 1,668 miles to go. Our bodies and spirits were holding up well as we approached the halfway point of the race.

When they told us the plains were flat farmland, they were not kidding. They were *plain.* As someone who enjoys a lot of visual stimulation when I ride, this got incredibly boring incredibly quickly. We approached Kansas, which is known for its boring landscape, tornadoes, wind, and friendly people. Every year, RAAM riders talk about Kansas, and every year the wind conditions change. We said a quick prayer to Flatulous, God of the Tailwind, that he would provide a much-appreciated push.

I saw the lightning in Kansas while we were still in Colorado. We were headed into a massive storm. It was dark, and the lightening was so pretty. An hour later, I was singing a different tune—this was the kind of storm I had only read about in books. The wind and rain were thrashing me all over the road. Jason was yelling at me in the radio. "Stay close to the white line!" The wind was blowing me over the double yellow lines, and I was having a very hard time controlling my bike.

Daylight came, and we heard that the night crew had found a Subway restaurant. This was a big deal; we had been dealing with eating McDonald's for what felt like every meal. Beau rode up beside me and yelled the good news out the window, asking me what I wanted. For some reason, I really wanted a meatball sub and cool ranch Doritos because, apparently, riding your bike for several days straight turns you into a stoned college student. I spent the next couple hours thinking about the culinary delight that Jason was going to deliver to me.

When I finally got my meatball sub, my first thought was, *"Where's the rest of it? Surely someone didn't eat the other half. This is not at all what I was imagining..."* That evening, when Jason came back on as my night crew, I let him have it.

"A six-inch sub?! I am riding my bike across the entire country and I don't get a footlong?!" I had never been so fired up about a sandwich before.

Jason started laughing at me. "We keep wasting food. I figured that was all you were going to eat!"

I was really irritated. Fortunately, I don't have a great memory, so I forgot about it pretty quickly.

Although we were racing as a team, Kacie and I had very little interaction with each other. In order to beat the record, someone always had to be riding. Whoever wasn't riding needed to be resting. We had practiced doing rolling exchanges during the day, where the second person starts off at a slow speed until both bikes' wheels cross. We were not really great at this. It was uncomfortable to stand half-clipped into your pedals, turned around looking for the other rider. The crew would tell me to take off and ride, but it was almost impossible to tell how fast Kacie was riding up to me. Our exchanges were the only time we interacted, and we had decided to make an animal noise to alert each other we were approaching.

It is really difficult to come up with *that* many animal noises.

We celebrated reaching the halfway point—Pratt, Kansas—with a short stop for a photo. I stuck a unicorn (my spirit animal) in the back of my top and took off for my next pull. I am fairly certain I was the only rider at RAAM that year who rode with a unicorn. Time station #26 was reached at 3 days, 22 hours, and 40 minutes. We were at the halfway point and still on target to break the record—1473.5 miles down, 1520.1 to go!

Leaving Kansas, we headed into Missouri, which was my least favorite state. This was the first place where it started to get humid. Up until Missouri, the heat was mostly dry. Now we were unbathed and sweating. The drivers were really aggressive and had no love for cyclists. There was a change of scenery with the Ozarks and more climbing. We also had a wonderful surprise visit from a friend named Angie, whom we had met at the Florida Double Anvil race. She asked what we needed and offered to go to the store to pick up some much-needed supplies. We were desperate for fresh fruits and any food *other* than McDonalds. Seeing Angie and her two daughters on the side of the road with signs and food was an awesome pick-me-up and greatly appreciated. At this point, we were riding solo, with not many other cyclists in site.

My tongue had started to get swollen, along with my gums, and my mouth had a very uncomfortable feeling. The inside of my cheeks felt like raw skin. I had consumed about 50 Uncrustables and figured it was too much jelly (because another thing riding across the country does is turn you into a scientist), but it kept getting worse—to the point where I could barely swallow.

I stuck my tongue out and showed it to Beau, who was navigating the van. "Hey, Beau, does my tongue look weird to you?" I slurred.

Beau's face recoiled in the horror that he must have seen. "Oh...I need to take a picture of that." He snapped a picture and texted it to a dentist friend in Atlanta.

A few minutes later, Beau told me that I had thrush. Oral thrush is most common in children and babies and is an overgrowth of the *Candida albicans* fungus, a naturally occurring fungus in our bodies. When your immune system is suppressed, this can cause an overgrowth of the fungus, which feeds on sugar. My inhalers to treat my asthma, combined with lack of sleep and sugary sports drinks and gels, made my mouth an ideal spot for the thrush to camp out and take over.

Thrush is *incredibly* painful.

Dr. Pate, the dentist Beau called, offered to call in a prescription for a medication that would cure the thrush. There was only one problem; he said it would make me dizzy. We couldn't risk me not being able to ride, so we got the medicine, but I didn't take it, and I guess we expected that to help somehow.

Kim, our massage therapist, had brought a bagful of tiny brown glass vials filled with various essential oils. Kim knew that oregano and lavender oils were natural antifungals. She whipped up a little concoction for me to swish around in my mouth. The taste was horrendous. But it wasn't worse than the thrush.

Every day, I would call my dad, who wanted a daily report of our progress.

"Dad, today isn't going so great," I reported. "I have thrush in my mouth. Have you ever heard of it?" My tongue was so thick that I sounded a little drunk.

"Hell, yeah, I know what thrush is! Had it in the Marines. Tastes like a bear shit in your mouth." Dad didn't miss a beat.

The mouthwash worked some, but not enough to make eating easy. Even drinking was burning my mouth. The crew had to work extra hard now to force me to eat. Every time I got into the van from a pull, they would make me eat something before they gave me my phone.

As the race wore on, we were sleeping less and less, and the effects of cumulative fatigue were starting to show. We were getting giddy and were becoming obsessed with finding the perfect spot to pull the van over and make exchanges. As we traveled farther east, the states were becoming more and more populated. This meant we had fewer good options for pulling over.

Someplace in Illinois, with less than 900 miles to go, Keith and Beau were looking for an appropriate spot to pull over. I had all my gear on, including my helmet with the radio. Keith pulled over, and Beau hopped out of the van. He gave us the thumbs down; the tall grass was keeping us from seeing the drop off. Beau started jogging up the road. He looked so funny I couldn't stop laughing.

He was wearing the receiving earpiece for the Cardo radio, which was instantly activated by my shrieking laughter.

"What are you laughing at?" he demanded.

I was crying I was laughing so hard. Keith was saying, "Look at him! He looks like a duck! QUACK, QUACK!"

Tears were streaming down my face I was laughing so hard.

Beau started laughing, too. "You want me to give you something to laugh at?" He dropped his pants and kept running, his white behind exposed for all of Illinois to see.

"BEAU!" I shrieked. "Nudity is against the rules! If we get a penalty, I will kill you! Pull your pants up!" We were all punch-drunk with silliness and sleep deprivation.

Any doubts I had about Beau's ability to crew were gone. He was rock solid and remains one of my favorite humans.

Each day found me excited to have marked another state off the list. Our crew was doing a good job of making sure we focused on what was directly in front of us. *Let's not think about the fact that you have 800 miles left; focus only on your three-hour pull.*

I am not a huge fan of knowing every detail about what is coming up. Either way, I have to ride it, so I told my crew not to tell me much about what was coming up. The one thing I did want to know was what state we were in.

Steve was my nighttime navigator. He and his brother Jason have a special relationship—the kind that includes a considerable amount of bickering back and forth. I wanted to know what state we were in, and Steve told me were in Illinois.

"Geez, we have been in this state *forever!*" I whined into the radio. "Are you sure we are in Illinois?"

Steve said, "Yep, I am sure."

A few minutes later, I radioed back in. "I don't think this is Illinois, guys. We were here all day. Are you checking the route book? If we are going in circles I will kill all of you."

"Disregard. We are in Indiana, not Illinois."

Whew!

Indiana became Ohio. I really liked Ohio, as it was very RAAM friendly. There were signs posted in people's yards and manned time stations. The rolling terrain and short climbs in Ohio reminded me of the terrain in Georgia. Kacie and I were still riding strong and on target to break the record. There was still one little thing we had to tackle— the Appalachian Mountains.

The hardest climbing in RAAM takes place in the last 320 miles of the race. I was starting to feel the cumulative effect of not taking in adequate nutrition due to the thrush. At one point, Emily was trying to keep my mouth open and squeeze peanut butter packets and pudding down my throat because swallowing was so painful. I was very, *very* hungry and beginning to hallucinate during my nighttime pulls.

Thankfully, my hallucinations were of the friendly variety. At one point I was convinced that the reflectors in the road were dancing fairies. I was laughing hysterically and begging the crew not to run over them. When I got back into the van, Emily handed me an Arby's sandwich and said, "You *have* to eat this."

I fumbled around with the sandwich, trying to eat it. Then I realized the best part was the cheese and Arby's sauce, so I just started licking it off like a two-year-old. Frustrated with my inability to eat the sandwich, Emily took it away from me. Thankfully, the crew found some microwavable rice that I could tolerate. Your body can do amazing things when you put your mind to it, like ride your bike 3,000 miles undernourished and sleep deprived.

As we approached the hills of West Virginia, we felt like we could climb strongly enough to break the record. We needed to remain strong day and night. This was also where we were beginning to catch soloist riders, who had begun their race three days prior to ours. When a team catches a solo rider, it is customary to not blow past them but gradually ease up on them and give them the respect they are due for tackling this incredible race by themselves.

With 180 miles to go, we were now in Maryland and would face the section RAAM describes as the most difficult part of the race. Known as the Four Sisters, these climbs are short, steep, and brutal. To the body that is already exhausted and nearly broken, it seems cruel to have to finish with climbs like this. Riders are warned they might have to come off their bikes and walk, which would be understandable at the end of a 3,000-mile bike race.

The climbs lived up to everything that RAAM described them to be. During my climb up the last hill, I started thinking, *this is it, it's all downhill from here.* I had abandoned the race radio in favor of an iPod in one ear. The sun was beginning to rise as I crested to the top of the hill. At that very moment the theme song of my life, *Good Life,* by One Republic, came on. I started crying tears of pure joy and gratitude. I have never been so thankful in my life. As I got to the top I started to hear the *naayyyy nayyyy!* sounds of a horse. A horse! I looked over to my right and saw crew member, Ben, in a unicorn costume, chasing me up the hill.

You might think Ben ruined the special RAAM moment I was having, but quite the contrary. It was absolutely amazing. The only thing that *might* have been better would be if someone simultaneously threw a glitter grenade at me.

As we continued toward Annapolis, we were still on track to break the record. Riding through the Civil War memorials in Pennsylvania, with tourists out snapping pictures and our crew in unicorn costumes and pink tutus, was quite the sight. The crew had endured eight days on the road, and it was wearing on them, too. They were growing weary and ready for a break.

Chasing the record was extremely motivating, but so was the fact I would get to see my dad at the finish line. I kept telling my crew, "I really want to see my dad," and every time a negative thought crept into my head, I thought about him waiting for me at the finish. Dad wasn't my only motivator. So were *swirly things*. Unable to think of the word *toilets,* I started saying I couldn't wait to see a *swirly thing* to use the bathroom in. Cross-country pit stops on the side of the road had grown old.

The finish line at Race Across America is at the pier in Annapolis and so incredibly special. Everyone gets their own time at the finish; there are no worries of being chased down in the finishing chute. In fact, they hold all riders up at a Shell gas station about six miles away, where your time officially ends. All two-person teams got 23 minutes added to their overall time, and we no longer needed to chase the record. We had made it. They said we had five minutes to "get ready" for our RAAM escort to the finish line. We washed our hair and used the *swirly things*, putting on fresh kits and wiping ourselves down with action sports wipes to *shower.*

We rode the remaining six miles together—really the only time we rode together the entire race. As we crossed the finish line, we heard our official time of 8 days, 2 hours, and 35 minutes being announced. Champagne flew through the air in celebration. My dad was out front in his *Power, Pedals, and Ponytails* shirt, along with the surprise of seeing Jason's parents and his closest Marine Corp friend, Kim. It was truly one of the finest moments of my life.

I was totally overcome with gratitude and appreciation for our crew. They sacrificed so much and believed in us every mile from Oceanside to Annapolis. Without them, we never would have made it out of California. I am still in total and complete awe that people, some of whom were strangers, could be so giving.

Participating in this lifestyle teaches me so much. I would be lying if I told you there were not conflicts or unpleasant situations throughout the race. It's impossible to put 11 crew members and 2 racers together under those circumstances and expect that everyone will get along the entire time. But what's important is that everyone prevailed past the adversity in the name of the goal. Witnessing such selflessness from my friends and loved ones was the greatest gift and life lesson I could have received.

Physically, my body was not as broken as I assumed it would have been. The thrush in my mouth went away fairly quickly after I actually started taking the medicine (who knew?). My right hip and knee hurt from using that side to climb into and out of the crew van repeatedly for eight days. I was tired but relatively not as sore as I thought I would be. In fact, I went running the week after the race. Its frightening, really, when you do things like this and a week later you can say, *well that wasn't "that" bad!*

The part about RAAM that was all consuming was the fundraising and publicity efforts. If I wasn't training for RAAM, we were hosting silent auctions, emailing people, and generally trying to get the word out there. That felt more exhausting for me than the training itself some days. Once I decompressed and everything was down, I was left with a bit of a *now what* feeling. I played around with looking for a few events, but nothing really stirred me up like RAAM had. Jason had sacrificed a lot to support me at RAAM, including his race season, so I was happy to take a break and step back to support him.

When you do something as large as Race Across America it is all-consuming. You live, eat, and breathe RAAM preparation for months. Then in eight days, it's all over, and you are left with virtually nothing to do. When you are used to training 25 to 35 hours a week, it can be challenging to take the break. Some people find themselves depressed and feel like they are in need of some type of goal, while others are burned out from the training and need the break to let their bodies and minds heal. I find it particularly difficult to deal with all my extra time and energy and often feel pressure to pick out another adventure because people are always asking, "What's next?"

If you want your body to perform at a high level, you need to allow it time to rest and rebuild. Allow yourself time to socialize, gain some weight, spend more time with your family. Should you stop training completely? Absolutely not! But an off-season is important, and if your body doesn't force you to recover by becoming injured, you run the risk of becoming burnt out. If your training and racing isn't fun anymore, then it might be time for you to take a break.

7

DREAMING BIGGER AND BIGGER

Our deepest fear is not that we are inadequate. Our deepest
fear is that we are powerful beyond measure. It is our light,
not our darkness, that most frightens us.

—Marianne Williamson

It's not hard for me to stay motivated. I love working out. Biking happens to be my favorite, but I enjoy variety, so it's not uncommon for me to switch things up when I am not training for something specific. Rowing, crossfit, HIIT workouts—as long as I am breaking a sweat and moving my body, it makes me happy.

There is a distinct difference between working out and training for a race. I'm okay working out for a couple months, but after a while what I want is to train; having the end goal is important to me. It's hard to find adventures that really speak to me. Some people enjoy returning to the same races year after year. Local races are fun, and a great way to connect and catch up with the triathlon community—but what I am looking for is something *big,* so big that it causes me to lose sleep at night.

I spent the majority of 2014 thinking about my training and racing: what goals I wanted to set for myself and what seemed like it would fit

was the color of coke. It was devastating to hear he couldn't continue, but we felt confident that the decision the medical director made was the right call, especially considering our experience with rhabdo after the Keys 100.

Not finishing a race (also called DNF, for "did not finish") is not uncommon in endurance sports. Every athlete will have bad days, and sometimes those bad days happen to be race days. This would be the first time Jason had not finished a race, and we worried about how he would react. *Would he be angry? Sad? Regretful?* To be honest, I didn't know how I would react, either. While it was disappointing, I wasn't upset—just thankful he was safe and okay. Our relationship does not include giving up, and we push each other very hard and even rib one another as a method of encouragement, but this was definitely the right call, so I decided I wouldn't scream "QUITTER" in his face this time. You know, because if he continued with the race, it could mean hospitalization or even prove fatal. I definitely didn't want him to think he had let anyone down, and part of me worried that he would be furious that they wouldn't let him continue.

DNFs can teach you a lot of things if you allow them to. What Jason taught me was that you can fail with grace. Failure is probably the most widely ignored opportunity to learn a lesson. You can externalize failure—*it was the weather, the trail was stupid, the dumb officials made me stop, my crew didn't blah blah blah*—or you can choose the more constructive option and *internalize it.*

This does not mean to beat yourself up—rather to honestly ask yourself what you could have done differently for a more successful outcome. If you're going to go through life blaming nature and other people when things go bad, that's up to you...but understand that nature and other people and all of the other external factors, while a very convenient excuse, have one thing in common—*you cannot control them.* But you can control how you prepare for them and how you react to them.

So there we were, pacers who had been training to pace, fully outfitted with enough food and water for 100 hours of racing, with nobody to pace. We could have tucked our tails and headed home, but why waste the opportunity to be a part of someone's race? Once we collected Jason and got some sleep, he told us we needed to go help people finish. We headed back out on the course to find someone else to help (see above statement about how to react to adversity). Our friend Lauren needed pacers, so we picked up shifts with her. We also adopted a random runner, Sean, who was racing without any crew. We had everything he could possibly need and were ready to pace, so why not? I spent 7.5 hours with Lauren in the middle of the night, speed hiking in Lake Tahoe. We watched the sun come up. It was beautiful. My sadness over Jason's DNF was lessened by helping Sean and Lauren get to the finish line. Jason's attitude was so positive around the entire experience. He managed to turn a failure into an opportunity to help others. We learned a lot from the experience.

I didn't want to take the entire year off from ultra-bike racing so I found a bike race in Borrego Springs, California, the World 24-hour Time Trial Championship, to be held in November 2014. Don't let the race name fool you; this was not a time trial or a championship, as there was not any qualification process to get in. The idea of calling something that is 24 hours long a *time trial* is somewhat funny to me. Maybe a *trial by time* is a better moniker. My plan was to work hard to get fast at the 12-hour distance and better my mileage from the Texas Tejas race I did in 2012.

Jason joked with me that flying to California for 12 hours of racing wasn't worth it. So I made a somewhat last minute decision to race the 24-hour race instead. I had done a handful of long rides but was focusing on shorter, more intense rides in an attempt to maintain as much speed as possible.

We flew into San Diego and made the 2.5-hour drive to Borrego Springs, a fun desert town that is part of the RAAM course. Driving down the Glass Elevator brought back some awesome RAAM memories.

There are things you can just *jump into*, like a 5k, or a pickup game of basketball. Then there are things you should really *train* for, like 24-hour bike races. While the race itself was awesome—mostly flat, windy, hot, free of cars, and well organized—my performance was not exactly my best. I had battled a sinus infection in the week before, so overall I just felt a little less stellar than normal.

The race began at 6 P.M. This format is popular in long-distance cycling events. It allows you to race at night without being as sleep deprived. The race would consist of 26-mile loops, and my crew of one (Jason) would be stationary, waiting in the pit area for me to roll through. Jason affectionately calls me the *Pokey Puppy*, after one of my favorite children's books. I can definitely be *pokey* at times, wandering aimlessly and not paying much attention. Usually, my pokiness ends the minute I get on a bike, but for some reason I was struggling to wake up my killer instincts. My pit stops seemed too frequent and leisurely. Jason was prodding me to hurry up. There was only one other female in the event, the legendary Seanna Hogan, the winningest ultra-cyclist (male or female) I am aware of. Holding the course record at RAAM, Furnace Creek, and countless other races, she was a formidable competitor.

Seanna took off fast from the start and pushed the pace. We were so close together on the first lap that I could hear her breathing. She seemed to really be pushing hard. When she pulled away from me, it didn't bother me a bit. She must have stopped at a point where I didn't, because I ended up ahead of her quickly. Jason kept trying to tell me she was right behind me, but my normal competitive nature seemed less interested in where Seanna was and more interested in the incredible animal noises I was hearing coming from the darkness of the desert. Soon my small lead turned into 10 miles, then 15.

I had a new bike with fancy hydraulic brakes that started giving me fits around the 12-hour mark, getting stuck every time I tried using them. This forced me to dismount and unstick them, only adding to my time off the bike.

Mentally, I remained in relatively good spirits for the majority of the 24-hour event. I think events that are time-based like this are much harder than something that's, say, 400 miles long. In a 24-hour race, you're on the course for 24 hours, and this can make it difficult to maintain motivation to stay on the bike. You can easily get 200 to 300 miles in and decide you are done, and your race is over. This event in particular was different, because there was a 12- and 6-hour option. The 12-hour racers began at 6 A.M. and 6-hour racers at 12 P.M. It was fun seeing some fresh legs out on the course after 18 hours of riding.

The wind started to pick up, which was causing a bit of a sandstorm. Eyes burning and unable to see, I pulled over and stood on the side of the road for a few minutes. I was starting to slowly lose interest in riding my bike. Twenty-two hours into the race, I stopped, sat down in a folding chair, and ate a burrito. Slowly I drank a coke and just took a minute to relax. I had crossed over the threshold of *having fun* to "*Can we please just get to the end of this?*" Regretting my decision to not put more time into training for the race, my body was aching at all my contact points. Time trial bikes are made for speed, and as fast as they can be, they aren't known to be comfortable. With very little change in incline, this was a course that was made to sit in your aero bars, which is what I did.

In the last 30 minutes of the race, I passed Seanna. She's definitely my ultra-cycling idol, so this was a huge deal for me. When the race was over, she congratulated me on my win and told me I had way too much energy. In a polite way, she was basically saying, "You didn't leave it all out there." She was right. It was my first 24-hour event, and I had no idea how to pace myself. At the end of the race, I still had too much left in the tank. I ended up with 420 miles in 23 hours and 47 minutes, which was good enough for seventh overall against the men and top woman (out of the massive field of two). I vowed that would be the last time I ever showed up to an event unprepared. I respect these races and distances too much and, quite frankly, it makes me irritated thinking I could have, should have, or would have done better had I done a better job preparing myself. That is internalization.

Although Jason had a great attitude about his experience at Tahoe, he was still hungry for something ridiculously challenging. I had been urging him to think about longer distance swimming. He was third overall at a 12.5-mile swim around Key West, despite the fact that Keith and I spent half the race fumbling around in our ocean kayak and running into him.

Like any good girlfriend, I started scouring the internet for potential races. Long-distance swim races are in some really beautiful places, and selfishly, they don't mean crewing for 24+ hours or running 20+ miles. I found an awesome event, the S.C.A.R. swim challenge in Arizona.

Jason was accepted into the race to be held in May of 2015. The four-day event would include four swims in four lakes: Saguaro Lake

(9.5 miles), Canyon Lake (9 miles), Apache Lake (17 miles), and Roosevelt Lake (6.2 miles).

Guess who had also signed up to kayak 42 plus miles. Yeah, that would be me. All four of the swims were beautiful and truly challenging. Day 3 was the hardest swim of them all. The Apache Lake course would be 17 miles with 15 to 20 mph headwinds. The winds were so bad that kayakers were getting capsized and tossed in the lake. My hat blew off my head and, when I turned the kayak around to get it, the wind blew me downwind so fast that, when I turned around, Jason had already swum out of site. One of the support boats threw me a small rope and dragged me back to him, 60° water splashing all over me as I tried to stay upright.

When I made my way to Jason, he told me to just quit; there was no way I could kayak the rest of the way. The idea of leaving him in the lake without food or direction wasn't going to happen. I buckled down and kayaked harder than I have ever kayaked before. We tied his feed bottles to the kayak so I could fish them in when he was done. After I would throw him his bottle, I would pick up the paddles and paddle so I didn't get pushed backwards while he was treading water.

I didn't dare try to eat or drink anything. I stayed focused on the kayak, trying to take deep, powerful strokes into the water. With a half-mile to go, the wind completely stopped. The lake turned to glass. I ate and drank and decided to put my iPod on. One Republic's *Good Life* started streaming into my ears. The sun started to set as Jason made his way to the *finish line*—a boat at the end of the lake. It felt like a perfect ending to such a hard day. Eight hours and 39 minutes of swimming, one of the most challenging accomplishments I have had the privilege of witnessing.

The S.C.A.R. swim challenge finale was a 10k nighttime swim. I watched little blinking lights fill up the small lake. It was such a fun way to end a truly remarkable four days.

I often say that each race we participate in is an adventure. We learn and grow from each triumph and failure, and this was no different. Watching Jason pushing through the water each day left me inspired to find an adventure that was far outside of my comfort zone.

I arrived back in Atlanta with an itch to get back into some serious training. My coach, Heather, had moved to Italy and wasn't coaching me anymore. I spent quite a bit of time without a coach, training for nothing in particular.

I needed a goal, and I needed a coach.

I had met Brent Pease through his racing. Brent's brother, Kyle, has cerebral palsy. They race together, everything from sprints to marathons and even full Ironman races. I didn't ask Brent a thing about what qualified him to coach me or his experience with ultra-athletes. I didn't care. Brent had heart, more heart than anyone I knew, and that was good enough.

Now I just needed to find a race—the kind of race that gave me chill bumps and made me lose sleep at night.

It was no coincidence that, soon afterward, I saw a post on Facebook encouraging athletes to apply to a race called Epic 5. I knew what Epic

5 was, having read about it in Jason Lester and Rich Roll's books. I distinctly remember telling Jason, "That sounds like a logistical nightmare," and it was. Consisting of five 140.6 distance races, one per day, five consecutive days in a row…with one catch—each race was on a different island, so you had to fly between the islands after each race.

It didn't take long for me to figure out that Epic 5 had never had a female participant or even an applicant. This just further piqued my interest.

There isn't a great explanation for why I suddenly wanted to do Epic 5. Something about an event being run by a woman and never having a woman finish it really bothered me. *It only takes one of us to do something, then the rest know it's possible.* That thought doesn't just apply to women—it's fairly universal. Once someone does something like, say, a skateboard trick or a running pace formerly thought impossible, it removes a mental barrier for anyone who cares to put in the work. *What would it feel like to be the one who makes it possible?*

My mind was made up; I wanted to apply for Epic 5. Now I needed to break the news to Jason.

I'm a dog lover and I have a tendency to find dogs—a lot. With three of our own, we foster them until we find them homes, but not before I disrupt the entire house with a mangy, flea-ridden houseguest who desperately needs a bath.

I sent Jason a text: *You love me a lot right?*

He quickly replied: *Oh my God, you better not be bringing home another puppy.*

Me: *What if it's the cutest teeny, tiny puppy ever?*

Jason: *I just changed the locks. Have a good one.*

Me: *Okay...so what if I didn't find a puppy but I found a race instead?*

Relationship hack: Races are always better than bringing home puppies!

Jason didn't quite understand my interest in Epic 5. "You don't even like one Ironman...and now you want to do five in a row?"

"Well, not really in a row...I mean, they're on consecutive days, so you have time at night to...fly to the next race..."

He had a point. Never mind that I had no clue how to train or prepare for the race. Although he didn't totally understand *why* I wanted to do the race, he still gave me his blessing and support. That was the most important part of deciding whether to attempt it. We do not race without each other's support.

I sent Coach Brent a quick text: *Five Ironmans in five days. One on each of the five islands of Hawaii. Crazy?*

He responded: *Epic 5? DO IT.*

Wait...Brent has heard of Epic 5? It wasn't exactly a mainstream event. Only seven people had finished it successfully. It was surprising that Brent had heard of it. Surely this was a sign.

I floated the idea out to some friends, secretly hoping someone might talk me out of it. I made sure to tell them all the cons of the race; it was too expensive, too much of a logistical challenge, too hard to train for with my job. Every objection (excuse) I came up with was met with an enthusiastic response of, *"If anyone can do it, you can!"* Sometimes I really feel like I should re-evaluate my social circle. You know, have a few friends who see things through a lens of reality.

I sent my application in and waited. Events like Epic 5 are invitation only. Not because they are trying to be elitist, but because a participant who has not met certain requirements and is without adequate experience can be very dangerous. At the end of the day, people don't like signing up for events where very few people finish, so making sure participants have a good chance of finishing is important. The longer the event, the riskier it can become as it relates to sleep deprivation. Race directors want all the athletes and crew to be as safe and successful as possible. It's hard to know what will happen to you after multiple days of racing, but the most responsible course is to accept only people who have proven they can take their bodies to such extreme limits and be successful with it.

Several days later, I received an email from Rebecca Morgan, Epic 5 race director, saying that she wanted to set up some time to chat on the phone. After our phone call, I received my golden ticket, an email inviting me to participate in Epic 5.

It was July of 2015. I had approximately ten months to get ready.

My run volume in July 2015 was around two to six miles per week. A big swim week would be 5,000 yards. That's *total* yards, not just one swim session! I was biking around five to seven hours a week, so I wasn't *completely* out of bike shape, but let's face it...I seriously needed to increase my training volume for a 703-mile event.

Coach Brent started working on a quasi-couch potato to a 703-mile training plan. We knew my advantage would be my ability to bike and handle sleep deprivation. I didn't have a great track record with running long distances, so this worried me some, but not enough to think that I couldn't complete the race.

The summer of 2015 was spent building my base as much as possible without getting injured. It was also spent doing things that weren't very fun. Like running five miles to the pool with a pack on my back, swimming, and then running home. The outdoor city pool didn't open until 12 P.M., making this an even more pleasant experience in the Georgia heat and humidity. Jason would offer me words of encouragement if I would balk at running in 100°. "You know Hawaii is hot, right?"

We have a "*you signed up for it, you don't complain about it*" policy in our house when it comes to training. We consider the opportunity to race and train as a privilege, especially considering people like the benefactors of the Kyle Pease Foundation, who may not have been blessed with the physical ability to do these things. With that mindset, we focus on how thankful we are that our bodies can tolerate such high volumes and intensity. We try to focus very little on the negative aspects of training and on all the positives instead. Like being able to eat two breakfasts before 9:00 A.M.

With winter approaching and my friends and training partners winding down, it was becoming quite apparent that I was going to have a rather lonely winter training in solitude. As wonderful as the Atlanta triathlon community is, we tend to shut down our outdoor bike riding once temps drop below 45°. The high humidity makes even the low 50s seem much cooler.

I was spending more and more time in the pool, and Coach Maria was working on perfecting my stroke. She would walk up and down the deck, telling me to swim big. "You're at Epic 4 right now, we gotta get this stroke to Epic 5 level." Finally. one day it clicked. "See? That's what I mean?! All these years and you are FINALLY swimming big!" *I hope this is big enough to swim 12 miles in 5 days,* I thought.

Once my form was good enough for Epic 5, Coach Maria started working on building volume. Walking up on down the deck, she would refuse to allow me to offer any excuses for poor form or cutting swims short. When master's practice ended, I would move inside. "That was a good set," Coach Maria would tell me. That made me feel good until she said, "Now repeat it backwards." My weekly volume continued to grow, and I was finally starting to feel like a swimmer.

My swim workouts continued to get longer and longer. Arriving on time to Masters was no longer an option. I needed to be there early and swim at least 1,500 meters before practice started. The pools are open to recreational swimmers as well as structured Masters practice. I kept noticing there was one older woman who was always there swimming when I arrived. We struck up a friendship, and I learned that Pat woke up at 4:45 A.M. to take the honors of being the first person in the pool. She chided me that I needed to set my alarm earlier if I had any desire to beat her. Of course, that sounded very vaguely like a challenge, and you know how that goes…

Operation *Beat Pat to the Pool* was born—4:44 A.M. wasn't early enough. Neither was 4:43 A.M. When I got up at 4:42, we both arrived at the same time, and she jumped into the pool first. That must be where the saying "that's dirty pool" came from. Or maybe it was from billiards. Nope. Had to be this. Not wanting to wake up a minute earlier than I had to, I kept slowly setting my alarm earlier and earlier. I even titled the alarm *Beat Pat to the Pool*. Finally, when I got up at 4:39 A.M., I was in the pool before Pat. Success! I enjoyed getting to know Pat and was impressed by her dedication to maintaining a workout regime that people half her age would find challenging.

Planning for Epic 5 seemed to be a much smaller undertaking for me than previous races. Unlike Race Across America, where Kacie and I would need a crew of 11, Epic 5 would be a much smaller-scale event. Jason and I decided that we would bring a crew of just two. The question was, who? Keith was my obvious first choice, but as a newlywed, he had priorities that didn't include island-hopping for 703 miles of racing with me.

Whenever people want to crew, I always ask them, "Are you *sure* you know what you are getting yourself into?" I am a firm believer in setting expectations and making sure that people are very clear about what type of commitment they are getting themselves into. Not long after I shared my intentions of participating in Epic 5 on Facebook, Hilary reached out to me and said that she wanted to crew. Hilary had never participated in an ultra-event in any way. She had absolutely no idea what was involved in crewing, what I would expect, or what we expected of her. Hilary just knew it was a crazy thing to go to Hawaii and race 703 miles, and she wanted to be a part of it. I didn't know Hilary very well, but what I knew about her was that she was a very enthusiastic and thorough participant in anything she set her mind to. That's the bulk of it—the rest can be learned.

We took Hilary to dinner one night, and over sushi, we tried to highlight what all the most horrible parts of crewing would entail. Nothing seemed to faze Hilary. She was laid back with a sense of adventure. Hilary was going to be perfect.

With Hilary and Jason set as my crew, my only job was to continue to train to get myself prepared for the grueling event.

Since biking was my strong suit, I naturally leaned more toward long rides than anything else. I may have started off as a triathlete, but really and truly, I am a cyclist at heart. The bike portion of a triathlon is almost always the longest, and I'm a firm believer that being a strong cyclist makes the run portion of a triathlon more tolerable.

As the weather warmed up and we got close to May, Coach Brent scheduled several large blocks of extremely long training to simulate the fatigue of racing five days in a row. This wasn't easy, since I continued to work full time, so I planned to take some vacation days around these long back-to-back days. We called them *training camps*.

One of my training camps took place in the north Georgia mountains. The Appalachians are no joke, and even the most seasoned and strong cyclist can struggle there. I had three days of long training ahead of me, and I figured it would be solo. Imagine my surprise when my friend Thomas, who lives in the mountains, offered to ride with me. Thomas crafted our routes for each day. He made sure that they included as much climbing as possible on roads that I had never been on. Bailing out wasn't going to be an option.

Day 1 started with Masters Swim, then seven hours on the bike. I had a two-hour run lined up for dessert. I had no idea why Thomas had agreed to ride with me until we got on the roads. His face lights up with pure joy when he's climbing those mountains. It was hard to *not* be excited about my weekend of training with him at the lead. Thomas had designed the course and promised it would be a wonderful frolic in the mountains. He didn't disappoint. Seven hours and over 10,000 vertical feet later, we were done. Now to top off my day with an hour run and finish in time for a shower and dinner before I repeated the efforts the following day.

When you go to bed after an almost ten-hour day of training, it can be really hard to know that you need to wake up and do it all over again. Days that long are mostly spent in solitude, I mean, there are usually only about five to seven people in the entire world who train for Epic5, and who else would want to work out for ten hours? Well, Thomas apparently did. The next day rolled around and he offered to ride with me again.

We climbed and climbed until we hit the seven-hour mark. This was the point I had told my brain we would be done. When we weren't done, my brain and body started to argue a bit. Thomas assured me we were just a few miles away from his house, but that is exactly what he had told me a *few* miles ago.

"Okay, we have two options at this intersection," he offered. "We can go straight, and there is a nice climb, or turn left, and its flatter. Which do you want to do?"

"Well, I want to turn left, obviously!" I replied.

We turned left. "Oh, yeah, this way is longer," Thomas laughed.

It was hard to be mad at someone who had graciously offered to give me a tour of new roads for over seven hours, two days in a row. After two days of ten-hour workouts, Brent gave me a shorter ride on day 3 to allow me to travel back to Atlanta. Most people dread going to work on Mondays, but for me it meant a day when I didn't have to train for ten hours, so Mondays weren't so bad in my book.

Between back-to-back training camps, swimming 15 to 20k a week, and working a full time job, I was beginning to get stretched really thin. In an effort to support me, Jason was picking up my slack on the home front. He grocery shopped, cleaned, and took care of my bike and the dogs. He made sure that I could devote every ounce of my energy to my training. Not once did he make me feel guilty for all the time I spent away from him, or my inability to have an even remotely intelligible conversation with him after coming home wiped out from a long day of training. When I felt discouraged about my training or progress, both Jason and Brent reminded me that I was going to finish Epic 5. They had no doubt, so why should I?

I managed to stay injury free during these long months of training. This was mostly due to the amazing care I received from my massage therapist, Eileen Steil. She would dig into me on a weekly basis, applying cups to my most challenging injuries. "You feel so supple," she would tell me. "You are really taking care of yourself." *Really? I thought, because I feel like I just got out of an industrial clothes dryer.* Having completed a double deca triathlon herself, Eileen was the most experienced female ultra-athlete I knew. If anyone was going to be able to prepare me for what my body was going to go through, it was Eileen.

The biggest setback I had prior to the race was a bout of nasty food poisoning that left me virtually unable to move for three days. I lost nine pounds and was weak as a kitten afterwards. Psychologically it was a blow—I missed a training camp for which I had planned to take Friday off work and ride 120 miles three days in a row. My mind started spinning, thinking about ways I could make the camp up. Coach Brent texted me to try and ease my anxiety, telling me not to worry; it was just March, and we were still all set with my fitness levels.

As the days counted down, my body continued to become more and more adapted to the volume. I was leaning out despite eating almost 5,000 calories a day. My energy levels were increasing with each passing week. I was beginning to wake up between 2:00 and 3:00 A.M., wide awake after only four hours of sleep. Eileen assured me that this was normal and my body's way of adapting to the training.

One of my favorite questions people ask is, "Are you ready?" Ultra-racing is mental, and if I *wasn't* ready, I certainly wouldn't tell anyone.

Sometimes I *am* ready for the training to be over; sometimes I wish I had more time. Mostly, I just don't want to think about it too much.

One morning, I was in the pool locker room getting ready for work. I was almost ready to start my taper, the ten-day period when my volume would be drastically reduced to allow my body time to rest and get race ready. Pat was there and was quizzing me. "So do you really think you'll finish?" she asked.

"Of course I will finish." I replied. She smiled at me. "I think you will, too."

As I opened the door to leave, Pat yelled, "I know you can do it!" My eyes got misty and my legs were covered with goose bumps. This was going to happen.

My last hoorah before leaving for Hawaii was a half-iron distance race. This 70.3 mile race, just to shake the racing cobwebs off. Eleven days before Epic 5, I had strict instructions to hold back, and race at 140.6+ pace. This was particularly hard after having a great swim, exiting the water in second place overall. *Patience, grasshopper.* I let ladies pass me on the bike. *This is a training day.* I repeated over and over. It certainly wasn't my fastest day, but it was a good opportunity to practice patience.

The next day, I was bragging to Jason about how wonderful I felt. He laughed. "Well, that's good, because you have to double it and do it five days in a row." *Oh, yeah.*

I tamed my pre-race and travel jitters by obsessively cleaning my house and packing. Jason came behind me and repacked. I separated all my outfits for everyday into gallon bags and labeled them individually. We went over gear lists over and over. I typed up care taking instructions and put together a binder with all the race details and information.

Now all that was left was traveling to Hawaii!

When you have to commit to an event so far in advance, it can be difficult to maintain the same level of motivation throughout your training. Mental fatigue, as well as physical fatigue, are both normal parts of training for long-distance events. You can make training easier for yourself by surrounding yourself with a core group of positive and motivating training partners. Make sure your family and friends understand your commitment to your training and avoid making you feel guilty. Every day, I listened to a motivation video on my phone, sometimes up to five times in a row. When I felt my energy starting to fade, I would repeat the words to myself over and over.

Quotes that inspired and motivated me were everywhere, like, "Our deepest fear is not that we are inadequate, our deepest fear is that we are powerful beyond measure." I even changed the wallpaper on my phone and my computer to a motivational quote!

Ultimately, you have to want success more than you want to sleep in, stay out late, or drink too much.

To quote my favorite motivational video, "Talent comes naturally. Skill is only developed by hours and hours of beating on your craft."

8
EPIC 5

*Beyond the very extreme of fatigue and distress, we may find
amounts of ease and power we never dreamed ourselves to
own; sources of strength never taxed at all because we never
push through the obstruction.*

—William James

Hilary, Jason, and I descended upon the Atlanta airport to make our
way to Kauai-Lihue three days before the start of Epic 5. Seventy-five
percent of the luggage we took belonged to me. I had spent days meticulously packing and checking items off my list. My clothing for each
day was separated into gallon Ziploc® bags and labeled. Trying to
maintain the "Ministry of Fun," I wrote funny notes on all my bags.
Day 5 run bag was labeled, *LAST DAY YOU EVER HAVE TO RUN AGAIN.* My
methodical packing in the days prior to the event helped to keep me
calm. My sister-in-law gave me a small stuffed unicorn for good luck. I
took a sharpie and wrote, *FOLLOW TO KONA* on her. We named her Epic
Ellie, and she would serve as my good luck charm.

We flew to Los Angeles and then caught a connecting flight to
Kauai. For all of the things I can endure, long-distance travel isn't
something I handle well; my body and brain don't like being con-
strained to a small seat. Restlessness sets in after a few hours, even with

the best books and games. Knowing what I was going to face when I arrived didn't help much, either. I tried hard to contain myself for the 13-hour trip.

The first thing we noticed when we landed was the humidity. The air was thick and hotter than what we had left in Atlanta. Epic 5 volunteers greeted us at the airport with cheerful, "Alohas!" and leis. We were in Hawaii! There was no turning back now.

We settled into our condo and almost immediately went to sleep. It was almost 4:00 A.M. local time, and we were exhausted. We needed to try and bank as much sleep as possible before the race began.

The six-hour time difference made it difficult to sleep in. I woke up early to the sound of light rain. After quietly making coffee, I snuck out to the back lanai to relax. The storm quickly passed, and a double rainbow emerged. It was the brightest and most beautiful rainbow I had ever seen. Surely this had to be a good sign! I spent some time reflecting by myself then grabbed Epic Ellie for some photos. Jason and Hilary woke up in time to admire the rainbow, and then Jason got busy putting my bike together. Jason and Hilary went out for a run while I did a short bike ride to make sure that everything was in working order.

I hadn't considered it beforehand (being preoccupied with a ridiculous volume of training), but the very small number of people who do Epic 5 makes the event very unique and familial. The original start list had seven athletes, but it had dwindled down to just four of us who arrived in Hawaii: Oscar, Carlos, Enrique, and myself. We gathered together for dinner and athlete check-in at a large rented house. I really stood out as the only female and the only person who didn't speak Spanish. I was also the only person carrying around a stuffed unicorn and taking pictures of it with everything.

I had some reservations going into the event about how I would be perceived, considering I was the lone woman in the event. My experience has been mixed as it relates to how men accept racing with me. Logically, I would think, *the course isn't any shorter for me than it is for them, and we all trained hard to be here. It's not like I got a special women's pass or something. I should be looked at as just another athlete here with the same goals as everyone else.* But that's logically...and it would be fair to argue that there isn't much logic in deciding to physically destroy oneself for more than a dozen hours at a time...or in this case five days in a row. Women make up an incredibly small portion of any ultra-event—the longer the event, the fewer women participate. Men dominate short course racing, as it's all about legs and lungs. Longer events take heart and tremendous patience. My experience is that women race patiently and smart, and that can make us top contenders in ultra-races.

Let me expand on that a bit. It isn't popular to say this, but I will, because it is a fact. Men and women are different from one another in millions of ways. Men are physically larger and stronger on average—this shouldn't be news to anyone. In fact, it takes more work for a female to run, swim, or ride the same distance as a man if all other factors are equal. For that reason (and surely as a result of evolution), women have a generally higher pain threshold and, by necessity, when we take on endurance sports, we need to approach it from a slightly different angle and race smart 100 percent of the time. I had spent almost an entire year calculating how I was going to accomplish this event, and I knew it would come down to mastery of myself at some point. I had no idea how right I was.

The other athletes and their crew were incredibly warm and kind to us. I felt like the outsider, but it really had to do with the fact I couldn't communicate with them in Spanish and nothing to do with being a woman. Enrique, Carlos, and Oscar were all accomplished Ultraman athletes who knew something that possibly only a dozen or so people on Earth knew—just how hard we had all worked to get here. If they were nervous about what we were about to take on in two days, it didn't show. I hoped my brave face was as convincing as theirs.

Harnessing my energy before races is something I struggle with. *Peaking* is the term that describes what all athletes look to achieve before their big races. You push yourself to the absolute brink of exhaustion, then you scale it back big time. We taper in order to peak. *Tapering* is the time before the race when you drastically reduce your volume and intensity. If you are tapering correctly, you will suddenly be filled with a tremendous amount of energy. Your body feels like it's in perfect working order. Personally, the large reduction in volume makes me restless and more hyper than normal, probably as a result of the aforementioned energy. I've suffered with insomnia off and on for years, and heavy training helps me sleep. The closer I get to events, the less my body will sleep. Often in my heaviest training weeks, I would find myself waking up at 2:00 A.M., completely awake and ready to start my day. When I take away the training volume, it gets even worse.

It was important that I stayed as well rested as possible. This meant I couldn't explore the gorgeous island of Kauai but instead had to spend as much time out of the sun and heat as I could. I realized that, in a way, I had already started the race—I was at the point where I couldn't make any mistakes, like eating or drinking the wrong thing or—definitely— getting a sunburn. I passed the time by writing postcards to everyone who had made a donation to my fundraising efforts for the Kyle Pease Foundation. Thanks to the generosity of my amazing community, this took me a several hours. I took breaks to make sure my hands didn't cramp up too badly, walked around, and got in plenty of fluids.

Staying out of the heat was tough, because the A/C in our condo stopped working. Hilary was all over calling the owner and getting someone out to fix it. There was no way we could rest or sleep without air conditioning in the Kauai heat. We were starting to grasp the fact that everyone here was on *island time*, which is charming when you're on vacation on an island but not when you are broiling in a rented house with the biggest event of your life looming over you. Hilary finally got in touch with him during his lunch break, and he said he'd come by when he was done in two or three hours. *Three hours for lunch?!* It was hard not to laugh at him. He was straight out of an episode of Cheech and Chong. After much huffing and puffing and a little help from Epic Ellie the unicorn, he managed to fix the air conditioning.

There was not a ton of prep work that Hilary and Jason needed to do before we started. We grocery shopped but didn't want to overbuy, knowing we would be on another airplane within an hour of finishing Day 1's race. You would think island hopping would be simple but it really took an absurd amount of planning. The race had provided us with a large cooler, which was very helpful, because we were able to pay a small fee and use it as checked luggage. The small interisland flights even allowed us to keep liquids in it, which was also helpful, given our lack of access to grocery stores once the race started. We bought enough Uncrustables to last a few days and some other essentials like Mountain Dew, Red Bull, and 5-Hour Energy. All other food items and crew snacks would need to be bought while we were racing.

It was hard to believe that we were already at the night before the race. I don't have any prerace rituals or things I have to do before I race. No special meals; I will tend to eat whatever I feel like eating. I tried to remain as calm as possible. Hilary and Jason were both excited but calm. We ate dinner early, and I pounded water like a diabetic camel, wanting to stay on top of my hydration. Careful instructions were typed out for the crew: what I liked to eat, how often to feed me, ways to encourage me, and all the notes and directions from the race staff with our flight and hotel info. We had no tactical plan for how to execute this flawlessly. No plan survives the first variable, and this race was about 90 percent unknown. So we took the opposite tack; the goal was to race smart, race consistently. Go slow, 15-hour days at least, and just finish. It might not be pretty, but I would find a way.

I forced myself to go to bed at 8:00 P.M., remembering the friendly competition with the lady at the pool what seemed like years ago, I set an alarm titled, *MAKE PAT PROUD,* for 4:00 A.M. This was about to happen.

DAY ONE: KAUAI

We woke up at 4:00 A.M., ate breakfast, and quickly packed our things at the condo. Our swim start was at Hanalei Beach, a short five-minute drive away. Arriving in the dark, we walked to the beach, listening to the waves slowly crashing against the pier. I got my wetsuit on and tried to explain to Hilary how to guide me on the paddleboard. Technically, this was the first time I would ever swim with someone next to me on a stand-up paddleboard. I told her what I thought she should do, based on my experience pacing Jason in the past. I wished I had taken notes in my head...but here we were.

Athletes, crew, race staff, and volunteers gathered together in a large circle on beach. We joined hands and were led in a *Pule*—a traditional Hawaiian prayer. With my head bowed and eyes closed, I reflected on what stood before me. *Seven-hundred three miles. Five days. You can do this.* I felt calm and peaceful and was reassured by that.

As I said before, I don't have any prerace rituals, per se. I take time to reflect on my journey to the start line. That in itself is always an accomplishment to me and has a calming effect by reminding me that I am prepared physically and mentally. I'd arrived in Hawaii after ten months of training injury free and in the best shape of my life. I also took time to think about the people who had supported me on this journey and made it possible. Jason, Hilary, Coach Brent, and Coach Maria. My Dynamo teammates and friends. My family and coworkers. When I stood on the beach in Kauai and looked at the pier, I was overwhelmed with gratitude, and I felt like I was surrounded by loved ones. Many people were in my corner and supporting this. It was time to make them proud.

At 5:55 A.M. on May 5th, we began Epic 5. No race chips or timing mats, just a simple 3...2...1...countdown from the race director, Rebecca, and we were off.

With only four racers, there was not a marked swim course. We were led out by a paddleboard. Each swimmer had their own support, Hilary being mine.

It was Hilary's first time on a stand-up paddleboard. *In the ocean— for 2.4 miles.* In retrospect, maybe a bit of practice would have been wise, but again, here we were.

She did great on the way out. I was swimming fairly close to both Enrique and Carlos, close enough that I could see their paddlers. When we reached the halfway point and turned around, we had a pretty nice gust of wind and current in our favor. I looked over and saw Hilary had fallen off and was laughing. I couldn't help but smile as I swam. I thought about Coach Maria. *Swim big! Find more real estate!*

Sixty-three minutes later, I was back on the beach and peeling off my wetsuit. Unlike a normal triathlon where I would try and get into and out of transition as quickly as possible, now I was taking my time. I took a shower outside, went into the community bathrooms, and did a full change into a cycling kit. While Hilary dried me off, I ate a banana then slathered myself up with sunscreen. Time for a 112-mile bike ride. I love bike rides! I wondered how much I would love them in a few days...

Each athlete was paired with a local volunteer to help guide us through the city. This was a godsend, as none of us was familiar with the crazy unmarked island roads, and we already had plenty to think about. Our volunteer was Kim. Enthusiastic and excited to be a part of the race, Kim would help Jason and Hilary by riding along in the car and navigating the course. The bike course was open to traffic, and it was busy, so the plan was that the crew van would drive ahead to the intersections of the turns and point me in the right direction. If I needed water or food, I would yell out what I needed and throw them my bottles. We had practiced rolling transitions where I would grab the fresh bottle from a crew member standing on the side of the road to minimize my stopping time.

It was heating up quickly in Kauai. After an hour on the bike, the temps felt like they had doubled. *Stick to your plan. Ride within yourself.* On a five-day event, the biggest challenge is pacing yourself. I was hyper-energized after tapering and felt incredible. It was hard to suppress the temptation to ride as fast as possible. This was a race, after all! At the same time, not blowing up the first day was pretty important to finishing the rest of the race. They called it Epic 5 *Challenge* and not a *race* for a reason. It was timed, but there were no awards—other than finishing. This emphasis on finishing and not competing was so different from what I was used to, but I welcomed the change in atmosphere.

Soon I found myself descending down a busy road that wasn't in the best shape. While I love riding on new roads, what I don't love is not knowing what is coming up. Before I could avoid it, I rode over a huge hole in the road. My bike and body shuddered under the impact, but thankfully I stayed upright. I looked down to make sure that my bottles were still there. A few miles later, I realized my front wheel was flat.

I pulled over when I saw my crew van. "My front wheel is flat," I said as I dismounted.

Jason quickly went to work removing the wheel and changing the tube.

Within a few minutes, the flat was fixed, and I was back riding. Less than three miles later, I could feel the air seeping out of the tire. *Crap. Crap. Crap,* I thought, as I pulled over. *We didn't have a plan, but even if we did, two flipping flat tires in the first segment would not have been part of it.*

"What's wrong?" Jason asked.

"It's flat again," I said.

Jason started inspecting the wheel. He called the bike mechanics, Colin and Mike, who were not far behind us in another van. They arrived within minutes. As we were looking at the wheel together, I noticed a tiny crack in the carbon rim. Carbon rims are light, expensive, hyper-efficient, and tough, but for all of their attributes, they have one key flaw. If the structure is compromised in any way (like a crack, for instance), they can fail in a spectacular and very dangerous way. They tend to crumble and shred into a million or so sharp, expensive pieces. *This was bad. Really bad.* "It's cracked, y'all," I announced.

During all my training and racing, I have flatted less than ten times in ten years. I flatted once during a sprint triathlon in 2010 and had the good fortune of racing virtually flat-free since then. It looked like my good luck had run out in a big way.

In all our packing and preparing, we had failed to pack a second set of wheels. It came down to space, and the extra wheels would take up precious space that we didn't have. We opted to take our chances with the assumption that the race officials might have an extra pair we could borrow in the event anything happened. But really, what could happen? I had raced thousands of miles without so much as a flat, so this would be no different, right? Wrong.

Once we realized the wheel was cracked, Jason went into total problem-solving mode. Years of being on the Atlanta Police Department and on the SWAT team have taught Jason how to deal with pressure. I tried not to worry; that was his job. Hilary encouraged me to sit in the car and get out of the sun. This was going to take a while. I had made it known before the race that I wanted to have an attitude of gratitude at all times, good and bad. I didn't lose it when I had to sit in the van. While Hilary started looking for local bike shops to call, Jason and the bike mechanics starting thinking about possible solutions. Kim, who lived on the island, offered her bike or wheels.

Our biggest challenge was the fact that my bike was an 11-speed. Kim's wheels were nine-speed and 45 minutes away. The local bike shops seemed unaware of what an 11-speed was. I could hear Hilary on the phone with them trying to explain that they did in fact exist.

One of the other competitors, Carlos, was close by when I flatted and offered us his spare wheel. We took him up on his gracious offer, hoping his luck didn't turn into mine and we both finish Epic 5 on unicycles. *Hey…endurance unicycles…now that could be…never mind.* Now we needed to retrofit my bike to work with a ten-speed wheel. This entailed removing my current chain and replacing it with a shorter one. Luckily, I had the best pit crew no money could buy.

I spent the time while they were working on the bike sitting in the van, eating a sandwich, and texting Coach Brent. *"I cracked the Zipp rim."* Not only had I ruined a wheel, it was a wheel that was loaned to me by my amazing bike mechanic, Allen. This race had just gotten a lot more expensive!

Brent remained positive and assured me everything would be okay. *"I will overnight wheels there if I have to. You will find a way."*

After nearly an hour off the bike, I was back in action. Climbing back onto the saddle and seeing my bike computer (which I had left on) was a little bit more than depressing. Every minute off the bike counted as a minute at zero mph, so my average speed got slower and slower. I tried not to let this get to me. *Remain positive.* I was grateful that I was back on the bike. I was even more grateful for my generous and new best friend, Carlos, and the fact that my crew remained calm under duress.

There was just one issue. We had a flight to catch. Catching a plane to the next race isn't something you really consider in a regular Ironman race.

In the weeks prior to the race, Rebecca had contacted me about our flight options for Day 1. This would be the only day when we raced and *then* caught a flight to the next island on the same day, which, when paired with my incredible change in luck, was adding up to be quite a problem. In previous years, they had done this for all five days. For obvious reasons, they had decided that wasn't a great idea, and flying in the mornings and then racing made a lot more sense. Rebecca gave me a few options for flights based on estimated finish times. I could do a 13- to 14-hour race and catch one flight, or a 15-hour race and catch a later flight. There was a third option in the event I needed more than 15 hours. Confident that I could finish in 15 hours with plenty of time to catch my flight, I chose that option. My confidence was waning.

I tried hard to not push it too hard for the remaining 65 miles on the bike. It was so hot now, and we were riding next to the beach so the wind was making things more difficult. Times like these are what differentiate endurance training. I had to fall back on what I knew. Anything was possible as long as I stayed in control. *Just do your thing. Calm down. You'll be fine.*

When we turned around and started back, the wind was thankfully at my back. I felt strong despite the heat and was smiling from ear to ear. The crew was doing a great job of keeping me hydrated; I was going through bottles much faster than anticipated, because my water was just getting too hot to drink. I was really enjoying the race now. The cracked rim was a distant memory. Kauai was absolutely stunning, and it was hard to not love a scenic bike ride.

I rolled in from the bike to a random grassy field in front of a gym. There was no great place for me to change, and the gym wouldn't let us inside to use the bathrooms. So I crawled into the van and tried to maintain my modesty as much as you can when you're wriggling out of a bike kit and into running gear. Hilary slathered me with sunscreen and prepared to take off with me for a few miles. I ate a banana, took my time carefully applying Body Glide® to my feet, and tried not to look at the clock.

My plan was pretty simple for the marathons each day—finish them. I'm not a real data geek. I race with a power meter on the bike, but it's mostly an afterthought. I don't wear a heart rate monitor. My most enjoyable runs are the ones where I just *go*. We had decided I would wear a simple stopwatch for the races and keep up with just my overall time. This meant I was running *blind*, with no information on my pace or distances.

Hilary and I took off at a modest pace. The run course in Kauai consisted of five loops in a mostly secluded industrial area. We saw Enrique finishing his first loop as I started. He was running strong and in good spirits. The course was totally exposed to the sun at this time of day, and it didn't take long for us to realize it was much hotter than we expected, especially without the breeze you get on the bike. I was roasting and asked Hilary to run to the crew van and prepare me an *ice burrito*. Ice burritos are a wonderful contraption we made out of cooling towels. The end was sewn up to hold ice (or salsa, if you're a purist). Filled up and dipped in cold water, you could roll it up like a burrito and tie it around your neck.

When Hilary returned with my ice burrito, I instantly felt better. She traded off pacing duties with Kim while Jason stayed in the van, and they drove up a couple miles. I had asked that anyone who paced me had better be a chatterbox, and Kim made a great pacer in this regard. The mom of four small boys, she had plenty of stories to tell me about how she got to Hawaii, her kids, her work, her family. It's incredible how you can meet someone for the first time and feel like you are instantly great friends within a couple miles of running.

The course was mostly flat, and as we progressed, the hills kept feeling steeper and longer. I was walking them and making plans for when we would start jogging again. "Just get me to that sign right *there*," I would say. Kim was encouraging and kept me moving on target with my plan. We were surprised by a random runner who tagged along with us for a few miles. He had read a post online about us being there and decided to come out to join us. He verified that the heat was more unbearable than usual that day, telling us it was the hottest day they had had all year. *"Thank goodness it's not just me,"* I thought.

As the sun began to set, I realized I was going to be cutting it quite close to a 15-hour race. Hilary was pacing me and doing a wonderful job for her first real crew gig. I was so impressed with how she had handled every ounce of challenges we had dealt with so far. She laughed everything off and assured me there would be a later flight if we missed the first one. Missing our flight and catching a later one would push back what little time I had to recover and sleep. I *really* could not afford to miss that flight.

There were no mile markers on the course, and no aid stations. Just four people out there walking and running from van to van. After each loop, a volunteer would mark it off in their log.

About 23 miles in, I was starting to get hungry, with the type of hunger that race food wasn't going to help. "What are my dinner options?" I inquired. We had been warned that places closed early. We needed to make plans for our food well in advance. I did *not* want to be left without food after 140.6 miles of racing.

Little things can make me ridiculously happy when I am racing, and finding out that the loops were 5.2 miles each and not 5 miles felt like I had won the lottery! This meant I was about to be 26 miles into the marathon and not 25! I was also quite conscious of the time. Hilary and Jason made sure I knew that I didn't have time for dilly-dallying after we finished. I needed to get changed and to the airport as quickly as possible.

The *finish line* consisted of race officials in folding chairs, with clipboards and watches telling me I was done. Fifteen hours and three minutes of propelling myself 140.6 miles with an unplanned hour-long stop meant I was going to be cutting this 9:56 P.M. flight pretty close. Hilary helped strip me out of my run clothes, and within ten minutes of finishing, we were in route to the airport. If T3 exists, I had set a record. It was only 3.5 miles away, so I feverishly shoveled chicken fried rice in my face and guzzled as much water as possible.

We arrived at the airport around 9:20 P.M. The ticket counter was struggling with how to charge us for our oversized bike bags and additional coolers. Having all the racers, crew, and race staff at once was definitely more than they were used to dealing with. After what seemed like forever, they got the charges straightened out, and we were cleared to head toward security.

There are many things that you don't feel like doing after racing for 15 hours and *running* through the airport to make a flight tops the list. Thankfully, our flight was delayed 20 or so minutes.

Epic 5 took over the 33-minute flight, and everyone tried to take a quick power nap. After landing in Oahu, we needed to collect our bags and bikes and get rental cars. This seemed to take forever. I used the time to unpack my NormaTec compression boots and get into them while we waited. I sent Hilary off in an attempt to find water. We made it to our hotel a little after midnight. Jason was very clear that I needed to go to sleep as soon as possible. I was still a little too wound up for sleeping after I showered and got into my compression gear, and managed to drift off for sleep around 1:30 A.M.

Three hours later, my alarm went off.

New day. New island. Same 140.6 miles!

DAY TWO: OAHU

Four-thirty A.M. came sooner than I was ready for. I rolled out of bed and assessed my soreness...not too bad, considering what I had put myself through the day before. We ate breakfast and made the short drive to Ala Moana Beach, where I met Jen, our local volunteer for the day. Jen was wearing a unicorn costume and had a rainbow painted on her cheek. Epic Ellie now had a human friend! We snapped pictures, and I instantly loved her.

I was sad to learn that Carlos had dropped out of the race, leaving Enrique, Oscar, and myself. Carlos graciously offered for me to continue to borrow his spare wheels and ship them back to him in Mexico. His two sisters were going to continue traveling with us, and we took them up on the offer of borrowing the wheels. When we had the wheel debacle in Kauai, Jason made plans to rent another Zipp race wheel and had our local friend, Chet, pick the wheel up for us and meet us at the swim start.

After a daily briefing and Hawaiian prayer, we started our swim around 6:30 A.M. The sun was coming up, and it was gorgeous. Ala Moana is a busy park, even at dawn, with people doing yoga on the beach, swimming, and running.

We stayed close to the shore and swam an out-and-back section twice. Because there were buoys already out there, and so many other swimmers and SUP'ers in the water, there was no need for us to have someone guide us. The water felt a lot rougher than it did in Kauai, and my swim was slower, despite my arms feeling great. I exited the water feeling good, and Hilary was waiting for me with my gallon Ziploc® bag marked DAY 2 BIKE. It was off to the public bathrooms where we went to shower, lube up, change, and eat.

Oahu is the busiest of the five islands, and even though we were there on a Friday after most people should already be at work, we still found ourselves in quite a bit of traffic getting out of the Waikiki Beach area. Oscar and I ended up stopped at a light together within the first several miles of the bike. Our crew vans were not allowed to impede the flow of traffic, so they would ride up next to us and yell the next turn out the window before taking off. Oscar's memory was incredible; he knew every landmark we were looking for. I was thankful for that!

Having a local volunteer who knew the course was helpful for Jason and Hilary. Jen literally lived *on* the course so, naturally, we had to stop there so I could use the bathroom, meet her adorable kids, and say hello to her parents, who were in town visiting! I hope her kids were not too traumatized by meeting the stinky sweatmonster from Georgia.

The temps were noticeably cooler than in Kauai. I was enjoying riding along the coast with the crystal clear water when I heard what was becoming the all too familiar sound of my wheel flatting. *This cannot be happening to me again.* I looked at my bike computer; 50 miles in.

I was on the side of the road looking at my bike when the crew van pulled over. I looked up at Jason. "I think I ran over glass," I said, as I looked at my totally deflated wheel. Hilary hopped out of the van and ran back in the direction I had come until she found a broken rearview mirror, the likely culprit of my flat wheel.

Attitude of gratitude. Stay positive. While Jason started trying to troubleshoot, I sat down for a minute next to the side of the road, looking out at the water. I couldn't help but to think about how fortunate I was to be there, in spite of the situation. Hilary snapped a picture, and I posted it on Facebook with the caption—*If you have to be stuck on the side of the road, make sure it has views like this!*

We replaced the tube on the bike wheel, and off I went. I didn't make it far before I heard a *clump.* I looked down to see that my water bottle cage and bottle were gone. *Awesome. My bike is actually falling apart!* The crew van was still close enough to me to retrieve it.

At the bike turnaround, I heard my rear tire deflating AGAIN. *How is this happening again?* I tried really hard to keep from throwing my bike into the nearest volcano. I worked too hard for too long to let mechanicals get in my way.

We discovered that the tubes we had didn't have stems long enough for the deep Zipp rims. This was a problem. I sat down in the van and took off my shoes and helmet. It appeared this was going to take a while. Colin, one of the bike mechanics, put my bike up on a tree where it hung, sadly, for a really long time.

Sometimes when chasing unicorns, you follow the horn too closely, and it punctures your tires. Apparently this was happening to me.

After 45 minutes, I could feel myself becoming anxious. This was a lot of time off the bike. At the 60-minute mark, it was everything I could do to not start freaking out. I had ridden a mere 56 miles, which is exactly halfway on the bike course. My day was nowhere close to being over. My bike computer stayed on, and I was watching as my average speed kept getting slower and slower. I went to the bathroom, ate a burrito, chatted with Hilary, texted friends on the mainland, and tried as hard as possible not to focus on the fact that my idea of a perfect race had been blown to smithereens.

Both Mike and Colin lived on Oahu and knew someone who might have the right tubes. The problem was that he didn't live close. It seemed like they were gone for an eternity before they returned and my bike was fixed.

I wanted to get back out there and hammer the remaining 56 miles when I saw my average speed had dropped to barely 11 miles per hour. Almost an hour and 45 minutes off the bike, and I was antsy. My brain told my body to simmer down. This was day two.

We were getting back into the Waikiki Beach area Friday evening, with rush hour traffic preventing me from going buck wild. Traffic lights and cars were in abundance, oblivious to us and what we were doing. We made our way back over Diamond Head, where tourists were out in droves for pictures.

I have never been so happy to get off my bike in my life.

Waiting for me in transition was Wayne, one of the kindest souls I had ever met. We met when we were in Hawaii for Jason's Epicman race. He came down to see me and gave me a hug. It renewed my energy and brought a smile to my weary face.

Our friend, Chet "The Jet" Blanton, had agreed to run the marathon with me. I had excitedly been telling Hilary about how wonderful Chet was and that she didn't want to miss the opportunity to get to know him, so she ran some with us. Jen joined us for the first few miles before going back to the van with Jason to rush to a local bike store and clean them out of their inventory. We were not leaving Oahu without being prepared for more flats!

The Oahu run course consisted of a half marathon course that we would loop around and do again. This meant the crew would need to drive along the course to crew me. Oahu is the busiest island, and crews would need to use extra caution and could only park or stop along certain sections.

Chet was full of colorful stories and anecdotes. His energy and enthusiasm for life are apparent to anyone who has ever met him. Chet pointed out celebrity houses, stopped with me on top of Diamond Head to take pictures, pointed out all the course markers from the Honolulu marathon, and generally tried to keep me from being disappointed that I wasn't moving faster. My back was seizing up on me, and I was suffering from terrible spasms every time the terrain changed. Thinking it was my fuel belt, I took that off, only to realize that made them worse.

At the halfway point, Jason told me we were close to a 7-Eleven. He asked me if I wanted something. Chet joked about a slushy. Suddenly a slushy sounded really good.

"Bring me the biggest cherry slushy you can get," I requested.

That cherry slushy tasted amazing. I gulped it down. The sun had long set, and Chet maintained the same energy and enthusiasm at mile 20 that he had at mile one. As we approached Ala Moana Park, I couldn't help but notice how many people were out drinking, walking, having a great time. I loved that they had no clue why I was jogging past them so late at night and eating salt 'n' vinegar chips while trying to shuffle/run.

I knew time was a precious commodity, so I asked what my post-race food plans were well in advance. Jason told me they had pizza for us. "I don't want to hang out at the finish, let's round 'em up and get out of there ASAP," I instructed him. We didn't have a flight to catch, but we also didn't have the luxury of wasting time socializing, either.

We finished, hugged Chet, paused for a quick picture, and were in the van in route to the hotel within ten minutes. I pounded as much pizza as I could while simultaneously peeling off my socks and shoes.

While I showered at the hotel, Jason broke my bike down and packed it up. Day 2 was done. I crawled into bed around 12:30 A.M., sat in my NormaTec boots for 30 minutes, and at 1:00 A.M., I set my alarm for 3:00 A.M. and promptly fell asleep.

DAY THREE: MOLOKA'I

Three A.M. came about six hours sooner than I was ready for.

Jason popped out of bed like a cannon had gone off. "Get up! Don't be pokey!" I stumbled out of bed and instantly realized I was starving.

The kind of hungry where you'd normally be nauseated, but then you're too angry to be nauseated and too hungry to be angry. Post-race famish, as I call it. I started scavenging around for leftover food and made myself a bagel with peanut butter. *I need to do a better job of getting calories in,* I told myself.

I felt confident that the $500 we had spent yesterday at the bike shop meant today was going to be my day. Like it was some kind of atonement to the bike tube gods. *Your body and your bike are both in perfect working order. You're thankful to be here, grateful for the opportunity, and going to have an amazing day.* Carlos had returned to Mexico but left his spare wheels with his sisters, and they were now in our possession. I felt confident that Moloka'i was going to be a great island. Just don't break Carlos's wheels.

We loaded our luggage and bike bag into the van, giving ourselves ample time to make it to the Oahu airport for our 6:00 A.M. flight. After making it through security, I quickly found a Starbucks, where I ate again, drank a latte, and filled up my water bottle. I was beginning to feel the effects of the extended time in the heat and aware that my body was signaling me to drink more. This would have been easy to accomplish except for the fact I had to give my water up to go through airport security!

The 28-minute flight wasn't enough time for me to fall fully asleep, but I still put my earplugs in and eye mask on to try and relax.

As I felt the plane descending, I opened my eyes and started the process of getting myself psychologically ready to race. It's not easy to go from relaxing on a plane to toes in the sand, ready to race in one hour.

Suddenly the plane stopped descending. I looked over at Hilary. "It feels like we are taking off again doesn't it?!" Hilary agreed. We looked back at Jason, who was asleep behind us.

The captain came over the microphone. "Sorry, ladies and gentlemen, but the weather is too bad to safely land. We will return to Oahu, where you will deplane. Sorry for the inconvenience." So much for my perfect day of racing.

I looked at Hilary. "Well, it is called Epic 5 *Challenge* and not Epic 5 Fairytale right?" She laughed as we posed for a selfie with Epic Ellie and posted updates on social media.

It turned out that Day 3 wasn't going to be flawless after all.

When we got off the plane, they asked us to take all our luggage, as they weren't sure this plane would be the same one we would return on. Weighted down with bike bags, coolers, and carry-ons—Epic 5 racers, crew, and event staff took over the small terminal.

I climbed into my NormaTec boots and tried to make myself comfortable. A light sleeper, I need total quiet to fall asleep. Even with earplugs in, I could easily hear the conversations around me. I closed my eyes nonetheless and tried not to think about the fact that we were stuck in the airport. I felt comforted that we were all in this dilemma together, unlike my previous days of flats.

After an hour of waiting, the race director, Rebecca, approached us. She said that they thought it would be another hour before the storm would be clear enough for us to make another attempt to land in Moloka'i. Between the airports, baggage claim, bike retrieval, and car rentals, we were not getting out of the airport and to the race as quickly as we had hoped. Our 7:45 A.M. start time was now looking more like an 11:00 A.M. start, and Rebecca wanted to know if we could just run to the swim start from the airport while our crews got the rental vans. The mileage would be deducted from our marathon later in the day.

The swim in Moloka'i would be different from the other four islands, as we were swimming in a pool. This had something to do with frequent shark sightings and also with the incredibly strong current. Both sounded like very valid reasons to swim in a shark-free pool with no current.

I had no problem running the 8.4 miles from the airport to the pool, except for one thing—I was wearing my bathing suit under my clothes—an idea I had come up with to save time once we landed and were trying to get changed. Rebecca laughed and said as soon as I found my running clothes, we would take off. "Look at it this way," Rebecca said, "you only have to run 18 miles off the bike and not a marathon!"

Your ability to succeed at events like this has a lot to do with your ability to adapt and overcome. When your first ten plans don't work, you'd better have an eleventh that you can develop and implement as the tenth plan disintegrates. Being adaptable and creative while maintaining a good attitude far outweighs physical talent in ultra-racing.

You should also be really good at finding stuff quickly.

We boarded the plane again and started our second flight for the day. Landing safely, I rushed off the flight to the smallest airport I had ever seen in my life; an airstrip really. I knew Moloka'i was the smallest island, with a population of only 8,000. For some reason, I still expected a standard airport and terminals. They rolled out our luggage in a large cart and left it outside by the plane. Hilary spotted my bag and quickly pulled it out, where we proceeded to open it in the middle of the *airport* and search for my running gear. Oscar and Enrique did the same. Changing in a small bathroom, I filled up my fuel belt and met the local volunteer for the day: Wil and his two kids. Wil would lead us in his truck, while the first event staff to get a rental car would catch up with supplies to refuel us.

The air was thick and muggy. Steam rolled off the wet streets as we prepared to start Day 3—over three hours later than planned. Enrique, Oscar, and myself lined up and began the 8.4-mile run to Cooke Memorial Pool.

We ran together for a mile or so, chatting about Race Across America, which Oscar was interested in racing. When we hit the first hill, I stuck to my plan and walked it while they trotted off.

It didn't take much longer for boredom to set in. I started singing Christmas music. It generally cheers me up and helps me to not focus too much on the task at hand.

Molokai looked very different from Kauai and Oahu. What I noticed immediately was that it was empty. There were very few cars on the street, and the island appeared empty. There are no traffic lights in Moloka'i, one major gas station, and very limited food resources.

I made my way to the pool and saw the local volunteer, Will, pointing me in the right direction. His young daughter started peppering me with questions, like "What's that tape on your leg?" and "Why are you wearing that thing around your waist?"

I answered her questions as I walked toward the bathroom to change. Wil said, "She's going to ask you a million questions. She's pretty excited to meet you. We are out here every year, and you're the first girl in the race!" It didn't occur to me that Epic 5 was likely one of very few races held on Molokai Island, so it was a big deal to get to come hang out with us and see a female race!

I changed into my swim gear and hopped into the pool. Jen, my wonderful unicorn friend from Oahu, had traveled with us to Moloka'i and would be my designated lap counter—possibly the most boring job on Earth.

My 50-meter competition pool at Dynamo had me pretty spoiled. This was an outdoor 25-yard pool, and it was blazing hot. I started swimming and found my rhythm quickly. I love pool swimming. After what felt like 1,000 flip turns, I stopped to see what lap I was on. Imagine my surprised when Jen told me that I was just at lap 30 out of 77. Had it really only been 1,500 yards?

I kept swimming and noticed that a little girl was having a birthday party in the pavilion next to the pool. Pink streamers and balloons were everywhere. I could see the kids playing in the shallow end of the pool. It felt so funny, racing in the biggest event of my athletic career and sharing the pool with a little girl's fifth birthday party. They were completely oblivious to us.

Hunger was beginning to set in. I stopped and looked for some food. I had not planned or asked my crew to leave me any water or food, as an ocean swim wouldn't warrant stopping, so why should a pool swim be different? I took a big swig out of a random coke I saw sitting on the edge of the pool. "UGH!" I spit it out. "It's hot!" The pool was starting to make the insides of my mouth feel thick.

Flip, flip, flip. I could see myself passing both Enrique and Oscar in the pool; that surely meant my swim would be over soon. After what felt like an eternity, I was finally done.

Jason asked me if I wanted Wil with me on the bike. I was confused... Why would the volunteer be with me? The last three days, they had lined up local cyclist to ride with us. This was likely more out of safety concerns than companionship. I really wasn't sure. *What if he rode too fast?* I didn't want him pushing me. Jason assured me that he would just ride next to me and provide me with some company. I agreed and went into the bathroom with Hilary to change.

When I approached my bike with Will, the first thing I noticed was his awesome and colorful socks. He seemed fun already. Then he said, "I was surprised to find out this was your bike." "What do you mean?"

I asked. Wil said that he looked at all the bikes and the gearing options, assuming mine would be the one with the largest cassette. He laughed when he realized that wasn't the case. I teased him, "Girls can be pretty good climbers too, ya know."

I quickly learned that Wil grew up in Georgia, in the same suburb where I work. Imagine traveling to an island with 8,000 residents and meeting the one person whose parents live 15 minutes from you in Atlanta. I was even more surprised to find out that we had some common bike acquaintances!

All my worries about riding with him quickly vanished. I found the island of Moloka'i fascinating and wanted to learn more about its history and how Wil got here from Atlanta. A mountain biker, he came to work at the Moloka'i Ranch, met a local, fell in love, married her, and settled into a job in the education system. Wil told me a story of the Kalaupapa Peninsula off the island, where people with leprosy were exiled during the 1960s. A handful of them still live there today, ranging in ages from their seventies to nineties. I was so curious about this and asked Wil a million questions. "Why would someone choose to live on a peninsula you have to get to by mule if they can leave now?" I inquired. Wil simply said, "It's their home."

The bike course was incredibly scenic, with winding roads that were so close to the ocean I thought we might get sprayed with water. The island is 38 by 10 miles, with just one main town, Kaunakakai. This meant the course got creative with some out-and-back sections, and we got to see all of it—several times.

It began to rain, and Wil cautioned me about the descents as the sun was starting to fade. I stopped to make sure I had adequate lights on my bike and put on a rain jacket. As the rain picked up, Wil assured me it was temporary; we were headed back to the opposite side of the island.

Moloka'i has no traffic lights, and it also has no streetlights. This made for some really interesting riding once it became dark. I am legally blind in my left eye, making my night vision virtually nonexistent. I really wanted the van to direct follow me as much as they possibly could. The serpentine roads meant we would have to make some turns ahead of the van in total darkness. On unfamiliar roads, with the sound of the ocean waves hitting rocks, I felt my nerves begin to show themselves. I became stressed out quickly. Wil calmly guided me, even though he was riding without a light himself. He knew the roads like the back of his hand.

Our ride ended at Hotel Moloka'i. I thanked Wil profusely for his time and apologized that we had gotten such a late start to our day. Hilary escorted me with my run gear to the bathrooms at the hotel. We walked past the outside bar, where I couldn't help but gaze wistfully at the people at the bar drinking beer.

My transitions were getting slower and slower. I would sit down to put a sock on and forget what I was doing and start eating a banana. Then I would remember that I wanted to take an Oral IV®—tiny little shots that were keeping me from cramping. This would distract me all over again. *What was I doing again? Oh yeah, sock.* Acute fatigue manifests itself in very strange ways.

It felt like we were moving really fast until I checked my stopwatch to see that we had been fumbling around for 25 minutes. We made our way out of the bathroom, where I was greeted by Epic 5 event staff. Since we had started our day with an 8.4-mile run, all we needed to do now was 17.8 miles. Everyone kept calling it 18. This was making me nuts. I kept asking repeatedly, "But its just 17.8 miles, right?" Two tenths of a mile is just over 1,000 feet, but at that point in the race, I wanted every inch of it.

It was late in the day, close to 10:00 P.M., and I was surprised to find Adam, who wanted to join us. "You know we are going to be out here all night, right?" I asked him. He didn't seem to mind. Adam's uncle told him to call him when he was ready for him to pick him up. Just like that, we were off.

Adam's parents grew up in Moloka'i, and he still had a lot of family there. He happened to be in town visiting his grandmother and stumbled upon Epic 5. We started off jogging slowly, and I was excited to share all the Moloka'i history I had learned with Hilary. Adam added stories of locals not wanting the island to become commercialized, so they would burn down cruise ports or hotels being built.

It didn't take long for my jog to slow down to a walk. Enrique and Oscar passed by us, looking much stronger than I felt. I was crashing, hard. My eyelids were getting heavier. I stopped to pee on the side of the road and suddenly found myself bent over the guardrail trying to go to sleep.

Hilary and Jason began OPERATION KEEP DANI AWAKE. They started loading me up with caffeinated drinks. It would help, but it was temporary. I was getting slower and slower. "Tell me stories!" I begged. Adam was pretty good at this, but in spite of their attempts, I was still falling asleep.

"I think we can interlock our arms, and I can walk with my eyes closed." I grabbed Adam and Hilary's arms and laced our elbows together. Closing my eyes, I started to drift off to sleep, wondering if I was breaking a USAT rule by sleeping while racing.

"WAKE UP!" Hilary screamed, startling me awake. Apparently, you cannot walk and sleep at the same time. Dang. And here I thought I had invented a whole new sport.

Adam had just graduated from medical school. I peppered him with questions about growing up, Moloka'i, and medical school. Despite our conversations, I was still struggling to stay awake. My thoughts were getting more bizarre, and I was having a difficult time coming up with the correct words I wanted to use.

"What's that stuff they give you to put you to sleep?" I asked. "You know, the stuff Michael Jackson took?"

Adam replied, "I think you are referring to Propofol?"

"Yeah. That. I've been *prowifflewaffled*," I slurred.

I was trudging along at the slowest pace I think I have ever moved as the miles slowly ticked away. Jason was driving next to us, playing music to try and keep me awake. I grumbled about how low it was when it seemed obvious that no one lived on these roads.

Hilary told me that there was a change in plans for our travel in the morning. Our original flight from Moloka'i to Maui had been cancelled. We would now catch a flight that was 15 minutes earlier to Oahu, then immediately catch a second flight from Oahu to Maui. My brain was too fried to comprehend what Hilary was saying. I just knew to follow their instructions and go where they told me.

After I felt like I had been moving for an entire day, I asked Hilary what mile we were at. Surely, since we only had to do 17.8 miles, we must be getting *really* close, right?

My heart was crushed to learn I had three miles to go. Then I made the tragic mistake of looking at my watch. It was much later than I expected.

Suddenly I was feeling awake, and upset. I started crying. I realized I wasn't going to have time to sleep.

Jason encouraged me to move faster. The faster I moved, the more time I would have to rest.

Hotel Moloka'i just wasn't appearing fast enough.

"Where *is* it? You said it was only 1/2 mile away." Either they were lying to me or the hotel was moving. There was simply no way I was going that slow.

Hilary told me that I had 2/10 of a mile to go—1,000 feet. Since I couldn't see the hotel, it didn't really seem like she was telling the truth.

Jason rolled up next to us in the minivan and handed me the driest burger I had ever eaten. I slowly tried to chew it enough to swallow it. I imagine it was several hours old at least and very overcooked. I gave up on the burger and ate the cold fries instead.

As we approached the finish, Jason told me, "You have 30 minutes before we need to head to the airport. Do you want to sleep in the van or take a shower?"

That was a no-brainer. I was going to sleep in the van. Hell, I probably would have slept in the shower if that was an option, or while being dragged behind the van in a shopping cart. I stumbled out of my running clothes and into a T-shirt and pants. I was gross, covered in sweat, and dirty from riding in the rain. I put my earplugs in and my eye covers on and quickly fell asleep.

We never saw the inside of Hotel Moloka'i.

DAY FOUR: MAUI

Thirty short minutes later, I awoke to the van moving toward the airport. Jason told me to stay asleep in the van as he unpacked all our luggage and my bike. He waited until the absolute last minute to return the rental van, forcing me to wake up and start moving.

My body felt heavy and deeply fatigued. My mouth was dry, and my stomach was empty and growling.

Exhausted *and* starving. My two favorite ways to be before a race!

I guzzled down the remaining water in our bottles as we made our way through security. Foolishly, I assumed we could refill our bottles on the other side at the water fountain. This was not the case. The small *terminal* was nothing more than a couple rows of seats. No bathrooms, no water fountains, no vending machines.

I laid down with my head on Jason's lap and my feet on Hilary to catch a quick nap. When I woke up, I was immediately hit with the feeling of intense hunger. We started going through our carry-on luggage in hopes of finding something to eat. Nothing.

Scott, an Epic 5 staff member, saw us foraging for food. He offered me a small package wrapped in foil that looked like a burrito.

"What is it?" I asked. Not that I cared. I would have eaten anything at that point.

He explained it was a *musubi,* a popular Hawaiian food composed of a piece of Spam on top of a block of rice, wrapped in dried seaweed.

It was the most delicious thing I had ever eaten. Salty and perfect. I scarfed it down, making myself even thirstier. I asked security if I could go to the bathroom. *If you can drink some water out of the sink, you will feel better.* They told me if I left I had to go through security again. We didn't have time for that. The plane was already running late, and I couldn't risk missing the flight.

When the time came to board our flight, I was so thirsty I could barely stand it. Immediately I asked the flight attendant for water. The inter-island flights were so short, they had small four-ounce water containers. I started filling my pockets with them. When they were full, I picked up my shirt, and she loaded me up with as many as I could hold.

I knew the other athletes and crew were as thirsty as I was. I walked down the aisle like the water fairy, passing out tiny containers to everyone who was awake.

We made the short flight to Oahu just in time to make the flight to Maui. My brain was so fried that I didn't remember we were catching a second flight until everyone got off the plane and started rushing us to another terminal.

There is always a battle going on between what your brain is telling you and what your body is saying back. My body was exhausted. My brain was telling it that I had to travel 140.6 miles all over again. I tried hard not to focus on the fact that I was racing on no sleep. *The swim will wake you up. Just get in the water. You will feel so refreshed.*

My brain was telling my body just about anything at that point. I smiled a big smile and thought about how amazing it was going to be to finish today and head to Kona. Epic Ellie had been getting her fair share of photo opportunities and Instagram followers. That unicorn wanted to get to Kona, too, and I was going to help her.

I was so appreciative of my crew and the amazing way that they had kept me motivated and moving. They had gotten even less sleep than I had, and done it all with smiles on their faces. It made it easier to not complain, since they weren't complaining.

When we arrived in Maui, I started the process over again of going from trying to sleep to trying to be completely awake and race ready. Our swim was to be located at Kamaole Beach Park. For reasons unknown to me, we were swimming in between two buoys right off the shore 18 times, or 9 out-and-backs.

I immediately noticed the whitecaps in the water and the wind. It appeared that the storm was following us. The water probably didn't look as rough as I thought it was at the time, but I refused to put my wetsuit on until I got confirmation from the lifeguard that we were, in fact, allowed to swim. No sense in wasting energy, right? Rebecca confirmed that we were good to go for the swim.

We did our morning ritual of gathering on the beach in a large circle for our daily prayer, then we were off.

My brain was right; the water was refreshing. The choppy waves rocked me around, and we aren't talking about the kind of rocking that puts you to sleep. I was wide awake and once again finding my groove.

Some people don't like laps. I love them—it gives me an interval, something with a definite beginning, middle, and end. I counted down the nine out-and-backs in my head. Nine, eight, seven, six, five, four, three...*wait, am I at three or four?* I stopped to ask one of the kayakers which number I was on. *Two...one.* I exited the ocean with more energy than I started with.

Hilary escorted me to the bathroom to change. This was our seventh transition together, and we were getting pretty good at it...although my cumulative fatigue probably wasn't helping. Despite our highly organized process, it still took us quite a while to get ready.

Some 30 minutes later, I was on my bike and ready to roll. My local volunteer for the day was Todd. He would be driving our van for Jason and Hilary. It surprised me to see Todd in the driver's seat, and I realized just how exhausted Jason must be to let someone else drive.

The wind had picked up. Todd assured me that I would not be battling headwinds the entire ride. I forced myself not to be skeptical of this; surely I would make plenty of turns and eventually have the winds at my back, right?

The beginning of the ride had plenty of climbing and lots of wind. There are very few times when I think my size gives me an advantage in triathlon, but wind is one of them. I found myself struggling more than I usually would. Deep fatigue set in. I spend countless miles riding in solitude during training and racing, but today I desperately wanted Wil riding with me again.

At mile 28, we made a left turn onto Hwy. 380 and into headwinds. I was climbing and battling the winds when I looked down at my bike computer—12.8 average mph. *Twelve miles per hour. At this rate you will be out here forever.* It was completely demoralizing. I pulled over. My crew van wasn't far behind, and they immediately stopped. Jason ran over carrying Carlos' wheels. He started to remove my deep dish carbon rims and replaced them with regular wheels, which were heavier and would be easier to use in the wind. I immediately started bawling.

"I can't do this," I said between sobs.

"Yes, you can." Jason hugged me. "You're the strongest person I know."

"I'm not strong enough!" I wailed.

"Here. Drink this 5-Hour Energy drink and we will reevaluate at mile 50. Todd said that the wind will die down really soon. We are only on this stretch for five miles."

Jason unscrewed the top off a 5-Hour Energy, and I guzzled it down. I got back on my bike and started pedaling. *"At mile 50, I am quitting,"* I told myself. *"You're tired. You can go take a nap, then fly to Kona and do the last day."*

For some reason, my mind drifted to Pat, from the pool, and the day she told me she believed I could finish Epic 5. What would I tell Pat about why I quit? I started repeating my excuse in my head. *I was just tired.* I visualized calling my dad, "Hey, Dad, its me. Yeah, I quit. I was tired." Even in my foggy mind, it sounded like what my dad would call *a piss-poor excuse.*

I did a quick systems check. *Legs? Heavy but okay. Feet? Swollen but still working. Upper body? Felt amazing. Girly parts? Tolerating the saddle.* Once I realized my body was fine, I knew it was my mental game that was weak. My mental game. As long as no bones were broken or muscles torn, my mental game is the biggest part of what got me here, and it was the only thing that could get me to the end of Day 5.

I needed to suck it up and get myself into a better place.

Todd was true to his word, and in five miles, Hwy. 380 ended, and we turned left onto Hwy. 30. The headwind was becoming a crosswind, and the course was flattening out. For the next ten miles, I pondered my physical state before determining I was fine. Nothing was wrong with me. I was just tired.

OF COURSE I was tired. I was on mile 500-and-something of a 700-mile race. But you know what? Everyone else was tired, too. Enrique and Oscar were tired. My crew was tired. The race staff and volunteers were tired. I wasn't special, and my tiredness wasn't unique to me.

You made it through three days and multiple mechanicals, and now you want to stop because you are TIRED?! You're ahead of the other two guys, and NOW is when you want to quit?

I called myself out, and it worked. I started yelling at the crew van. Eventually, Jason rolled down the window.

"Don't you EVER let me talk about quitting something AGAIN!!!" I screamed at him. He smiled back at me.

Not only was I wide awake, I was fired up.

I started to replay my training in my head. *Countless weeks of sacrifice. Getting up earlier than I wanted to. Staying late at swim practice. Four A.M. wake-up calls. Getting back on the bike when my legs were begging me to stay in bed.*

Most of you won't be successful because when you get tired, you quit. Most of you don't want success as much as you want to sleep.

My motivational video that I had watched hundreds, maybe thousands of times started playing in my head.

You got a dream, you gotta protect it. If you want something, go get it. Period.

You have to believe that something different can happen.

I started yelling, "Dani Grabol will be the first woman to complete Epic 5!" Over and over again. Thinking I was talking to them, the crew van pulled up beside me.

"Everything okay?" Jason asked.

"Dani Grabol will be the first woman to complete Epic 5!!!" I screamed at the top of my lungs. Jason smiled. "Yes, you will, babe."

To be able at any moment to sacrifice what you are for what you will become.

I continued to scream. An hour later, I was still repeating it, over and over again. Two hours turned into three. Todd was right. The wind had died down. It rained on us, and then the sun would shine bright. The course was magnificent with gorgeous ocean views. Todd knew these roads like the back of his hand.

Jason pulled up next to me.

"In about a mile, there is a big pothole in the middle of the lane, so move over to avoid it," he told me.

By that point, I wasn't even questioning how Todd knew everything. I felt so lucky to have him in the van with us, warning me of every obstacle that could potentially cause my bike harm.

Stopping at the turnaround point, I dismounted so Jason could outfit my bike with lights. I spent a few minutes eating a delicious burrito, spilling beans and rice on my bike. I had done a complete 360 from mile 28 to now. A couple hours of positive self-talk and I felt great.

Most of the bike courses were out-and-back, so we didn't see much of the other racers or crew. I saw Enrique shortly after we turned around, and Oscar not long after that. It felt good to exchange a smile and a wave with them and to reassure myself that I wasn't the only person out there struggling with the exhaustion that four days of racing brings. I was looking forward to Day 5.

The sun set, and the crew van was shifting over and tailing me closely so I could use their headlights to see. Todd continued to give me a heads-up about every inch of the road; even in the darkness of night, he still knew precisely where every dip, hole, crack, and debris in the road were.

We followed the signs toward Wailea, and before I knew it, my fourth day of riding 112 miles had come to an end. It was hard to imagine in the darkness of the beach parking lot that I had swum 2.4 miles in the ocean that morning. I felt like I was in a time warp of sorts; it was passing so slowly yet so fast at the same time.

I had plans to meet a local triathlete, Jodi, who was going to run with me. Jodi and I were Facebook friends, having connected while I was training for Race Across America. The owner of Salty Coconuts, an apparel company, Jodi had graciously sent Kacie and me triathlon kits for ourselves and clothing to auction off at our fundraisers.

As I changed in the parking lot, Jodi pulled out clothing she had brought for me. For whatever reason, this made me ridiculously happy. She stuffed it in my suitcase, and I couldn't wait for the race to be over so I could dig through the goodies.

Hyperconscious of the time, I asked Mike, the bike mechanic, if I was going to get to sleep tonight. "Not if you have another night like yesterday." Ouch. He wasn't being coarse, he was telling the truth. I needed to move much faster than I had in Moloka'i if I wanted to see a shower or a bed. Suddenly both of these became very important to me.

Jodi and I took off. The run course consisted of two out-and-backs. We didn't have any real specific plans for how often the crew van would meet us to re-up supplies. Immediately I could tell that I liked Jodi a lot. She had a tremendous energy about her. Jodi was really fast, like Kona-qualifying fast. I had warned her my pace would be a slow jog at best. Jodi kept me moving and distracted, telling me stories about her life and how she made it to Hawaii.

It didn't take long before Enrique passed me. We spent a few minutes running together and exchanging pleasantries before he took off.

"You can catch him," Jodi told me. Nothing about Epic 5 was competitive. Our times were being recorded, but with three participants there was clearly never going to be a winner. I assumed every day I would be the last to finish, and for three days I was. I told Jodi that Enrique was leading every day.

You have to believe that something different can happen.

I don't recall exactly what it was that Jodi said to me, or how she said it, but she effectively told me that I could absolutely run harder than I was running, and that I was stronger than I was acting like I was.

I passed Enrique, and we ran together for a couple miles. He offered me some coconut candy, and I offered him some salt 'n' vinegar chips. Whether the guys had intended to or not, I had felt like the odd one out. *Only female. Only American. Only person who didn't speak Spanish.* I might have been paranoid, but I didn't think they took me seriously. (This might have had something to do with the fact I was carrying a stuffed unicorn with *"FOLLOW ME TO KONA"* written on it.)

Maybe Maui would be the day I wasn't going to be last to finish. I didn't feel particularly competitive about the event, but I had three days of mediocre races, and I needed to prove something to myself.

Between the promise of a shower and bed at the finish line and the thrill of being in the lead, I moved much faster than I had in Moloka'i. I maintained my lead and arrived at the Maui Banyan Hotel, where Rebecca was crying, telling me how proud she was of me.

She had no idea I had tried to quit earlier.

We checked into our room to find that Rebecca had done all our laundry. I took a hot shower for much longer than I should have and crawled into bed. It had been 281.2 miles of racing and too many flights since sleeping in an actual bed.

One hour later, my alarm went off. Epic Ellie was headed to Kona.

DAY FIVE: KONA

We arrived at the Maui airport to find it almost empty. With extra time, I took my NormaTec boots out of my backpack and carefully crawled into them. We had made it. We were going to Kona. I felt very energetic despite the lack of sleep. Jason tried to tell me to take a nap, but I felt like a kid on Christmas Eve. I called Coach Brent and my dad. It felt so good to hear my dad's voice. I fought back tears as I tried to minimize how exhausted I was to him.

Mother's Day had fallen on Day 4 when we were in Maui. For the ten years I have been racing, I have missed eight Mother's Days due to racing. This year, my mom decided to come to me, with my younger brother in tow. They were in Kona waiting for us.

Other Epic 5 crew and race staff started to trickle into the airport. The air felt light. A burden had been lifted off of us, and we all seemed to be smiling more and happy. We had made it. *"Just one more Iron-man"* seemed like an absurd statement, but that's what we were thinking.

Enrique sat down next to me, and I encouraged him to use the Nor-maTec boots while Hilary pulled out her grandma's sewing kit and started to do some minor procedures on my blisters. I hadn't really had much time to pay attention to the state of my feet. They looked like two dead animals. Riding and running in the rain had not bade well for my toes. I already struggle with swelling in my feet after long events, and this time was no different. I tried not to focus on them. I just had one more race left, right?

Landing in Kona felt so good. I had envisioned the Big Island would be full of scantily clad triathletes, swimming, biking, and running all over the island, because Kona exists for triathlons, right? Imagine my surprise as we drove to the swim start and it looked like a regular Hawaiian island.

My mom and brother greeted us as we arrived at the Kailua pier. I looked at it skeptically, wondering how in the world this was the start of the Ironman World Championship race. It looked like it could barely hold 200 swimmers at most.

Today's start felt more casual. We were taking our time changing in the bathroom, not having to worry about starting later than we planned. We had no flight to catch after this race. Not having that pressure made me much more relaxed.

My mom followed Hilary and me to the public restroom and started chatting with us, as if we were casually catching up after not seeing each other for a week. I found it mildly entertaining that she was more interested in sharing stories of my brother attempting to surf than making sure I got ready for the swim.

The swim in Kona would be the exact one that thousands of Ironman World Championship racers before us had swum. A simple out-and-back, with the promise of colorful fish sightings and possibly sea turtles.

We gathered on the beach for our final Hawaiian prayer, smiled for the camera on the beach, then off we went. The water was murky and choppier than I anticipated. We had plenty of support kayaks in the water that day. I had asked my support to please stay close to me; I have a hard time seeing out of my left eye. I wanted her to guide me as straight as possible toward the buoys.

I was having a hard time finding my red kayak. The choppy water and currents were pulling us too far apart for me to site off her. I would swim several strokes then look up to see her farther away. This made me think I was swimming off course, which was really frustrating. The truth is that, when it's windy, it's more difficult for the kayakers to stay on course. Swimmers catch far less wind in the water than you do on a kayak.

The swells got larger, and Enrique and I were stopping at almost the exact same times to make sure that we were both still on course. I kept yelling at my kayaker, "Closer! Please! I can't see you!" If I weren't so completely exhausted, I probably would have realized that she was keeping her distance to keep from unintentionally running into me with the kayak. It was comforting that Enrique and I were so close to each other, and I reassured myself that we were both on course.

We must have passed about 100 buoys, or at least it felt that way. Enrique stopped at one buoy and questioned whether we were supposed to turn around. I heard him and stopped swimming. *This has to be the turnaround,* I thought. Nope, "keep going" the kayakers told us.

When we turned around, the current seemed to be taking us sideways. For my fifth day of swimming 2.4 miles, my arms felt surprisingly great, it was general fatigue my body was struggling with. Exiting the water, I saw Enrique on the beach pointing at his Garmin and saying that we had swum long. By Day 5, every inch made a difference, mostly psychologically.

T1 took place in the public bathroom like it had four times earlier. My transitions were getting longer and longer as the days went by. The more I tried to hurry, the more I started to forget things. Hilary had fine-tuned the process of reminding me to apply sunscreen, making sure I ate, put on deodorant, and, most importantly, applied anti-friction cream.

The Big Island is famous for its lava fields and heat. I was prepared with cooling sleeves for both my legs and arms. I slathered myself in sunscreen. Lyndsey, a local cyclist, was leading me out as the first person to start the bike course. We were riding the Ironman World Championship course, and I was excited to see what all the fuss was about.

A light drizzle started to fall as soon as I got on the bike. "Don't worry, it never rains on this side of the island for long," Lyndsey told me. After a couple miles, he said he needed to head back to get Enrique and Oscar. He gave me the next couple turns I needed to make.

Have I mentioned that I am terrible with directions? Well, imagine, if you can, trying to remember turns when your brain has been replaced with cotton balls. Miraculously, I made the turnaround where Colin and Mike were waiting. I handed off my sunglasses to them, and they instructed me to turn right at the Shell gas station.

The rain was coming down more steadily now, keeping my cooling sleeves damp and doing their job. I made the right turn and saw a couple more race volunteers who gave me some instructions for my next turn.

I totally missed the turn. The road got really steep really fast, and empty. My gut feeling was that I was going the wrong direction. I also felt like Jason and Hilary should have been someplace with the crew van. So if I was going the right way, I would see them soon. *Ride one mile then turn around.* After a mile and no crew, I turned around and rode back to the light. Thankfully, I saw Enrique on the other side of the road in the left hand turning lane. I yelled across the busy intersection at him, "Is this our left turn?" I was pointing in the direction I thought we needed to go. He nodded yes. I made my way over to the far lane to turn right (since I was coming from the wrong direction!). I caught up to Enrique, who was still smiling but not happy about swimming long. He gave me the distance his watch said we swam, and in my head I was thinking, *"I am pretty sure that's 2.4 miles."* But my cottonball brain just nodded with him in agreement. I pulled away and saw Jason and Hilary shortly after that.

"Where were you guys?! I got lost!" Jason told me that they had not planned on being at that intersection. With that many lights and traffic, it would have been nearly impossible for them to safely stop and give me directions. I assured him I wasn't mad at them; just wanted to let them know they needed to keep a close eye on me. Simple instructions were morphing into complex calculus in my brain.

We were headed north on the infamous Queen K Highway. The rain stopped, and the sun began to shine. Kona is notorious for its heat, which rises off the black lava fields. In preparation for this, I made sure my cooling sleeves included SPF protection. When sprinkled with cold water, they kept me cool while shielding my arms, neck, and shoulders from the sun.

The bike course seemed much easier than it had in previous days. I was giddy with excitement. We had followed Epic Ellie to Kona, and we had made it. The Epic 5 crew was waiting for us at the bike turnaround in Hawi; this seemed like the first real *town* I had seen once we left Kona.

As we closed in on the final miles of the bike course, I peddled harder and harder to finish before the sun set. My body felt like I was easily pushing over 20 mph, but I would look down at my computer and be sorely disappointed in my actual speed. I was developing hot spots in my feet from the continuous daily pressure of the pedals. The rain left me damp, and the friction from riding in the rain in Maui was becoming increasingly uncomfortable.

We arrived back at Kailua pier to change, in the public bathrooms, for the last marathon. Twenty-six and two-tenths miles was all that separated me from becoming the first woman to complete Epic 5! I fumbled around, trying to move quickly but feeling very disoriented about what I needed to do next. Hilary helped me as someone came to lock the bathrooms up for the night. "Please don't lock me in here!!" I yelled. "I am just changing for a marathon." I giggled at how casual I sounded.

For someone who isn't really a runner, setting out for my fifth marathon in five days was quite an effort. Honestly, I can't remember the last time I ran over 100 miles in a *month,* much less 131 miles in five days.

My body quickly reminded me that I was not in fact a runner. It didn't take long before my feet were throbbing from the hot spots and blisters. It started raining (so much for this side of the island never getting any rain!). Jason had decided that he was going to pace me for the entire run in Kona. This would be the first time he had ever paced me in a race.

"Can you tell me a story?" I asked him.

"You know I am not good at telling stories," Jason replied.

Instead of telling stories, he kept trying to push me to go faster. Like a kid who doesn't want to go to bed, this was just making me push back and whine. Unlike Maui, where the miles ticked away effortlessly, in Kona, I felt like I was slogging along *so slowly.*

Enrique caught up to us, and soon so did Oscar. This surged a bit of competitiveness in me, and I caught up with them. We ran together for a while. It felt so surreal that three athletes from three different countries with three different backgrounds were together on their last day of racing running almost side by side.

Out of almost nowhere, I was hit with total delirium and hunger. Every time I saw the crew van, I wanted something to eat.

"You aren't hungry," Jason told me. "You just ate."

I started to whine like a three-year-old. "But I ammmmmm hungryyyyy! I am soooo hungry. I didn't like what you gave me to eeeeeaaattt."

Jason told the van driver to drive farther up the road, knowing I wouldn't know the difference in seeing them in one mile or five.

Totally unable to focus on the task at hand, I asked Jason if we could start calling people. I was looking for stories any way I could get them. I called Coach Maria and could hear the surprise in her voice when she answered. "What are you doing?" she asked. "Oh, just walking. I am at mile 18. I am starting to go a little crazy." This wasn't news to her, and she laughed at me.

It rained off and on for most of the marathon. The mist kept me awake and painfully aware of the blisters that I had developed in Maui. Around mile 20, I was convinced my feet were broken. Jason kept telling me over and over that it would be almost impossible for me to be walking on broken feet. Hilary hopped out of the van and joined us.

"Guys...I know this is going to sound weird, but I don't know whose legs these are. Like...I know that I am not an alien, and this is my body, but these aren't my legs." I had lost every shred of sanity. Hilary and Jason laughed at me.

The last few miles are a blur. I was hallucinating pretty badly. I saw animals that weren't there. Thought all the cars were trying to hit me. At one point, I even saw a Japanese man sitting in a car yelling at me. (It was a hat sitting on the dashboard, and it didn't answer me when I apologized.)

My feet were now in excruciating pain, and I wanted nothing more than to change my drenched socks and shoes. Laser-focused on the finish line, Jason refused to let me stop. "It's just going to be a waste of time. It's still raining, your feet are just going to get soaked again."

He was right. *Plus, my feet were broken into a million tiny pieces and, obviously, my soaking wet shoes were all that was holding them together.*

As we approached the finish, I wanted Hilary and Jason to finish with me. I mustered up what last amount of energy I had left to *jog* to the finish. There was no timing mat or hundreds of people cheering for us. No one putting a medal around my neck and announcing my name. Instead there was my mom in her pajamas, crying hysterically, fumbling with her phone and trying to take a video. (She filmed herself instead.) Some race staff were there, some weren't. Oscar was sitting on the pier, speaking on the phone in Spanish. It was so simple, yet I fail to find words to describe how I felt. I had done it.

THE AFTERMATH

Taking my shoes and socks off was a traumatizing and horrific sight. I ate something that I don't remember tasting good or being nearly enough to satiate me. Gingerly, we made our way to the hotel.

Coach Brent was texting me and telling me that a local news station wanted to interview me. Not tomorrow, but immediately, so go take a quick shower and connect with them. *Really?*

With Jason passed out in the bed behind me, I managed to figure out how to download Skype, set up an account, and connect with the news station. They requested I move around a bit, fix the lighting, angle my phone differently, find a towel to prop it on. With each request that required me to move, I groaned in pain. The interview turned out to be hilarious, mostly because they were filming the sound bites of me groaning and played them.

My social media accounts and text messages were blowing up. I had voicemails galore. I tried to shut myself down and rest. I was so uncomfortable. The swelling in my feet was unreal. I dozed off around 4:30 A.M. with my legs propped up on all the pillows I could find.

Two hours later, I woke up in the most horrible pain I have ever felt. It shot through my legs from my hips to my feet. My knees and feet hurt so badly that I didn't even think I could walk. I stood up and starting crying. *You have really done it this time. Your feet are broken for sure.*

My sobbing and groaning woke Jason up. "What's wrong?" he asked. "My feet hurt so bad. I think they're broken."

"No, they're not. You're fine." Jason rolled over and was back asleep in minutes.

He was right (again). I was fine; more than fine, really. In the next few days, the swelling went down, and blisters popped. We snorkeled with sea turtles, saw black sand beaches, and hiked by gorgeous waterfalls.

CONCLUSION

This Marianne Williams quote stayed in my bathroom for months for me to read daily. *Our deepest fear is not that we are inadequate, our deepest fear is that we are powerful beyond measure. It is our light, not our darkness, that most frightens us.*

It is petrifying to proclaim to everyone you know that you are going after some big, lofty goal. I wondered what people would think of me. Would they think I was ridiculous? What would happen if I failed?

Then I thought about my work with older adults. I used to work in a retirement community. Every morning, residents would gather in the library to drink coffee and chat. Often, their casual conversations would turn into reminiscing. I would listen to them talk about missed opportunities at work, places they never traveled to, things they wished they had said to their parents before they passed. As I listened to them, I couldn't help but wonder if I was living a life that would be filled with regrets or one I could look back on one day and think, *"I did everything I wanted to do within my capabilities. I took risks, I made decisions. Some were good, some were bad, but either way I owned them."* I decided that the only thing I ever wanted to regret was missing all the good season finales on TV.

Someone who once smoke and weighed 220 pounds and struggled to walk up a flight of stairs without getting winded was now capable of completing 12 miles of swimming, 560 miles of biking, and 131 miles of running in five days. This journey was not always easy. Was I afraid and fearful at times? Of course I was. But I made a decision many years ago, when I was overweight and miserable—I was going to believe in myself. If there wasn't a way, I would create one. I would not become a victim of my circumstances. I wouldn't offer up excuses for why I didn't look the way I wanted to look, or why I wasn't the person I wanted to be. I would create my destiny through the decisions I made, and above all, I decided I would be grateful for the gifts I have been given.

ATTITUDE OF GRATITUDE

What is an attitude of gratitude? For me it's a conscious decision to be grateful for what I have, the gifts I have been given, and my capabilities. Complaining is so effortless for so many of us that we find it difficult *not* to do it. When I was a child, my mom would say, "Stop being an ingrate," and I had no idea what that meant. As an adult, I completely get it! *There is always something to be grateful for.* Yes, you might have had a horrible day. Your body might hurt, your heart might be broken, things won't always go your way. Focusing on what is wrong will only make those feelings stronger. Instead, try focusing on what is *right.* When you complain, you give the people around you permission to complain, too. Before you know it, you will be surrounded by negativity. Try going a week where you have to mention something you are grateful for every time you complain. You will feel so much better. There are so many things in this life we cannot control, but our daily outlook on life is something you can determine. *Choose to be grateful.*